Creating
REAL ESTATE
Connections

*Combining 500 Years of Forward-thinking
Real Estate Experience and Strategies.*

By Allan Dalton

with Gee Dunsten

TownAdvisor

Rumson, NJ

ISBN-13 978-0-692-37393-4

Printed in the United States of America.

Dedications:

Allan Dalton's dedication:

To my wife, Carol, our three daughters and nine grandchildren.

To Dale Stinton, Bob Goldberg, Richard Smith, Ron Peltier, Dave Liniger, Gary Keller, Alex Perriello, Pam O'Connor, Bruce Zipf, Steve Morris, Tami Bonnell, Gino Blefari, Sherry Chris, Phillip White, Budge Huskey, Rick Davidson, Charlie Young, Joel Singer, Jim Weichert, Wes Foster, Dick Schlott, Ed Krafchow, Chris Mygatt, Realtor.com, RIS Media, The Real Estate Book, Pillar to Post, Brad Inman, Steve Murray, and all other leading brokers, brands, media companies, State associations, and (most of all) individual Realtors® who create value-added Real Estate Connections throughout their career...for making the Real Estate Industry as great as it is.

With deepest gratitude to North America's builders and developers and mortgage companies, for providing a reason to create Real Estate connections.

Special thanks to my mentor Joe Murphy.

In Memory of Bill Kiley.

Gee Dunsten's dedication:

To my wife, Susan, our five children and four grandchildren.

To the National Association of Realtors® for all they have done to help me flourish in my career. I'd like to extend additional gratitude to all my fellow CRS Members, and past and present CRS instructors.

In loving memory of Howard Brinton, my eternal mentor, for the elegant and respectful way he influenced the lives of thousands of Realtors® through teaching NAR® courses and creating Star Power...a network that will never be duplicated.

Foreward
by Allan Dalton
Co-founder, TownAdvisor.com & Former CEO of Realtor.com

As a kid growing up on the streets of Boston, I was once warned, "Allan, don't mess with those guys... they're connected!"

"Connected" back then sounded foreboding, but today as an adult the degree to which one is "connected" within one's local communities can immensely shape one's professional destiny.

Indeed Real Estate Professionals owe their success to whether or not they can make and sustain connections within their communities.

Moreover, the creation of local offline connections is considerably more attainable than "owning" online connections.

To do so however requires: education, systems, and a community business plan.

This book is dedicated to helping community centric Real Estate professionals become the first and last point of contact with prospective homesellers within their local communities.

To accomplish this lofty, relevant and timely task I have asked some of the most credible and accomplished community centric Realtors® in North America to significantly contribute to *Creating Real Estate Connections* and share their legal "insider information."

I am confident that readers of this book will see their careers transformed.

Allan Dalton

Acknowledgements:

I extend my deepest appreciation to Gee Dunsten, and the highly impressive *Creating Real Estate Connections* community of authors, for their invaluable collaboration in making this book possible.

I also would like to thank Stefany Sheridan, Terry Carey, T.J. Golding, Connor Berscha, Guy S. Nembhard, Jr., and Melissa Pilgrim for their significant contributions.

My greatest gratitude however is reserved for Thomas Ryan Ward for devoting his exceptional structural, design, and organizational excellence – as he masterfully managed the entire process required to bring Creating Real Estate Connections to life.

– Allan Dalton

About the Authors:

Allan Dalton:

Allan Dalton has made a significant impact on the Real Estate Industry. A former president and co-owner of a 32-office Real Estate Brokerage for twenty years, Allan went on to create and develop national marketing systems for Better Homes and Gardens Real Estate, Century 21, ERA, and NRT-Coldwell Banker.

After the sale of the company he co-owned with partner, Joe Murphy, Allan worked for the Realogy Corporation – first as an Executive Vice President at NRT, then as a consultant to three Realogy brands, and finally as Executive Vice President of Coldwell Banker New England.

Most widely associated with his years as CEO of Realtor.com and president of Move Inc.com's Real Estate division (in charge of overall real estate operations), Dalton was named by the National Association of Realtors® as one of the Industry's 25 most influential thought leaders.

Dalton is also the co-founder and past president of RIS Media's Top 5 in Real Estate – where he authored the bestselling book, *Leveraging your Links*.

Allan has been a keynote speaker at countless Real Estate conferences throughout North America and abroad.

The co-founder & president of TownAdvisor.com and the Strategic Advisor to HouseFax.com, Dalton played professional basketball in Greece and is a former Boston Celtic draft choice. Allan and his wife, Carol, reside in Westlake Village, California, and are blessed with three children and nine grandchildren.

Legendary Industry coach, Mike Ferry, dedicated his book to Allan.

Gee Dunsten:

Gee Dunsten stands alone in the Real Estate Industry in the following way: for thirty years he has been the exemplar of how one can contribute at the highest level to both consumers and clients alike in his Ocean City, Maryland market, while at the same time, earning widespread admiration as one of North America's most credible, respected, and distinguished educators.

As a past president of CRS (Certified Residential Specialists), an exalted educational and referral-based network of industry-accomplished Realtors®, Dunsten has taught courses in all fifty states, numerous countries, and is a sought-after keynote speaker.

Known for his 'kinder and gentler' approach to delivering transformative information, in both an inspirational and entertaining fashion, Dunsten is hugely popular with the many friends he has gained from his more than 2500 local real estate transactions.

Gee, remains as active as ever in his local market, yet still manages to selectively present his incomparable level of industry-based knowledge for CRS and other high-impact Industry events.

Gee holds the following designations:

GRI (Graduate of Realtors® Institute), CRS (Council of Residential Specialist), MilRES (Certified Military Residential Specialist), and is the president of the Certified Community Marketing Specialist^{SM} online course, leading to a CCMS^{SM} designation.

About the Book's Publisher:

Larry Vecchio:

Larry Vecchio, whose chapter on regarding "Helping Communities Storm Back" after Natural Disasters appears in this book, is the co-founder of TownAdvisor.com.

Larry has been serving New Jersey's coastal communities with high distinction for decades through his conglomerate of real estate-related companies and services.

A noted and celebrated community activist, Larry was an inspiration for *Creating Real Estate Connections* and this book would not be possible without his support.

Creating REAL ESTATE Connections

Chapter 1 – Don't correct Competitors! Let Them Continue Offending* Consumers!   11
by Allan Dalton

Chapter 2 – Don't Just Differentiate… Distinguish Yourself.   33
by Gee Dunsten, *past president of CRS and prolific educator for the Real Estate Industry*

Chapter 3 – Creating Community Business Partners Through Sharing Success.   43
by Julie Vanderblue, *president of The Vanderblue Team – Higgins Group – Christie's Affiliate*

Chapter 4 – How to Become a Luxury Market Leader: an interview with Jack Cotton   55
by Gee Dunsten

Chapter 5 – Fighting for (not against) For Sale by Owners and Expired Listing Homesellers! *(Scripts Included)*   62
by Allan Dalton

Chapter 6 – Working Only w/ Homesellers Through Local Media & Marketing: an interview w/ Russell Shaw   74
by Gee Dunsten

Chapter 7 – Advocating for Your State: an interview with Rei Mesa   83
by Allan Dalton

Chapter 8 – How Community-centric Systems Grew my Company from 5 to over 50 Offices.   92
by Allan Dalton

Chapter 9 – Creating Connections with Out-of-State Buyers and Sellers   103
by Pam Charron, *exclusive TownAdvisor representative for Sarasota, FL*

Chapter 10 – Serving the "Celebrity" Community: an interview with Valerie Fitzgerald   108
by Allan Dalton

Chapter 11 – When Community Properties Become Distressed: an interview with Brandon Brittingham   113
by Gee Dunsten

Chapter 12 – Strategically and Sensitively Serving Seniors: an interview with John Riggins   123
by Gee Dunsten

Chapter 13 – Military Clients - how to serve those who have served: an interview with Alexis Bolin   130
by Gee Dunsten

Chapter 14 – Embracing Diversity – an interview with Teresa Smith   136
by Gee Dunsten

Chapter 15 – Creating Connections Through Local Community Organizations: an Interview with Leon Lopes   141
     by Gee Dunsten

Chapter 16 – Seasonal Communities/Second Homes: an interview with Linda Rike   146
     by Gee Dunsten

Chapter 17 – "Helping Communities Storm Back" after Natural Disasters: an interview with Larry Vecchio   153
     by Allan Dalton

Chapter 18 – Unlocking Gated and Golf Communities: an interview with Jack O'Connor   160
     by Gee Dunsten

Chapter 19 – The Don'ts & Do's of Creating Customized Community Videos   169
     an interview with a practitioner panel by Allan Dalton

Chapter 20 – Creating Community Websites: an interview with Rich Deacon & Thomas Ryan Ward   180
     by Allan Dalton

Chapter 21 – Ski Resort Properties: an interview with Steve Chin   189
     by Gee Dunsten

Chapter 22 – The Role of Social Media in Marketizing Communities: an interview with Michael Oppler   195
     by Allan Dalton

Chapter 23 – Creating Real Estate Connections and Referrals Through Industry Associations: 201
interviews with Anita Davis, Becky Boomsma, and Robert Morris
     by Gee Dunsten

Chapter 24 – Creating Corporate Relocation Connections through World-class Service: 211
an interview with Pandra Richie
     by Gee Dunsten

Chapter 25 – Marketizing Your Community: Creating Clients for Life.   217
     by Allan Dalton

Chapter 26 – Fighting for your Communities: Changing 'Ambush Alley' to 'Realtor® Respect'.   224
     by Allan Dalton

Chapter 27– Creating Your Community Business Plan and Selecting the Right Coach   230
     by Allan Dalton

BONUS Chapter 28 – Staying Safe... Professionally.   249
     by Allan Dalton

Check Out These Resources, Programs and Services   259

Chapter 1

Don't Correct Competitors!
Let them Continue Offending* Consumers!

by Allan Dalton

Co-founder, TownAdvisor.com & Former CEO of Realtor.com

As North America's most prodigiously Photoshopped profession...

(with apologies to Hollywood)

I respectfully suggest that the Real Estate Industry also devote <u>equal or more attention</u> to *how we sound* when seeking to *Create Real Estate Connections*.

"...if thought corrupts language, language can also corrupt thought."
— George Orwell

The Industry's Challenge is Not Your Ethics... It's Our Ethos

The Real Estate Industry has impressively evolved over the past decade in becoming more "high-tech" in how we professionally serve consumers and clients. These contemporaneous skills, along with how Realtors® swear to a Code of Ethics, leaves one to wonder: Why (according to national polling) are other similarly vital professions seemingly accorded more respect from consumers than the Real Estate Industry is? To me, this "respect disparity" is not a matter of *Ethics*, intelligence, hard work, or competence but rather *Ethos*. That's right "Ethos" and not "Ethics." For one is bound by Professional Ethics but not by Industry-wide Ethos. The Real Estate Industry, unwittingly, has created a communications Ethos that I wish to respectfully challenge. To that end, none of my following so-called transgressions (a word I specifically chose to dramatically call attention to this issue) represent Ethical violations but rather (to me) violations of Ethos.

I hesitated to begin this book with this chapter as we are in a time where the web, contact management systems, and overall technology are the Industry's main focus and not face-to-face communication. Yet I could not get this thought out of my mind. It has to do with, when I ask at seminars, "What percentage of your income is derived from how you communicate?" The answer is always, "one hundred percent!"

The reason why this important question surprises my audiences is because the Industry is overwhelmingly more dedicated to "what we need to do" versus "what we need to say." To demonstrate this, the next time you visit a convention exhibit area take note of how many more booths are devoted to how to connect with consumers through technology versus how to create more and deeper Real Estate connections through face-to-face and written communications. Clearly our concentration on "high-tech" has left the concept of "high-touch" in the dust! Consequently, this monumental imbalance (in my view) needs to be addressed by all of us. That is why this is my first chapter.

Transgression #1 – "Let's Take a Look at the Comps!"

Essentially, 100% of your competition assaults homeowners systematically by astonishingly employing the use of the words "Comps" or "Similar Homes." Whomever the coach or trainer was who first suggested this strategy – if they were here today – I would ask him or her this question: "What were you smoking and what cloud were you on to think that homeowners would ever willingly capitulate to the notion that there are other homes sprinkled throughout the community that remarkably – or, better yet, conveniently – are just like theirs?"

"I have two sets of 'COMPS' to review with you this evening. One shows SIMILAR HOMES to your home, the other shows SIMILAR CHILDREN to your KIDS! Isn't this exciting?"

Illustration: Ward/Dalton

How could anyone not fully anticipate that each and every time a homeowner is hit with the concept of "Comps" (meaning comparables) that every single homeseller in North America replies in the same fashion, "But they don't have five bedrooms," "But we have a new kitchen," "But we are closer to the high school," or other disdainfully stated corrective comments.

What homeowners are really thinking is, "How could we ever list our home with – or accept any pricing or marketing suggestions from – somebody who clearly isn't able to ascertain the distinctiveness of our lifestyle and who is actually comparing our home to the properties that we also could have bought? Furthermore, I bet this Real Estate Professional hasn't even been inside all of these other homes."

Alternative Approach:

"Folks, just so you know, each and every home is unique. That said, let's take a look at properties that buyers will also be evaluating at the same time they are viewing your home. This way we gain a greater sense of buyer behavior in today's marketplace."

Transgression #2 – "You can Trust Me!"

The next time you overhear a fellow professional actually say to a Consumer or Client, "You can trust me," whatever you do... do not correct them. If they haven't learned by now through the Realtor® Code of Ethics that trust is implicit (not only with the code, but with Agency, where it applies), they will never get this.

Alternative Approach:

When it comes to trust, trust is not an option. It's ethically what people are paying for... "Hello!" Let it pass, as a competitor might become defensive and might even think, ironically, that you are questioning if they can be trusted.

By the way, the greatest negotiating skills will always be found when one is acting fully upon Agency – as in most cases (but not all cases), it means that "You and your Client are as One".

Transgression #3 – "Let's see if we can Get You Qualified!"

While your Competitors want to create this officious and intimidating atmosphere by saying, "Let's see if we can get you qualified," here is your opportunity to say...

Alternative Approach:

"Let's get your purchasing power established, as that will help us in negotiations." Establishing purchasing power creates a completely different vibe than "let's get you qualified."

Transgression #4 – "May I ask for Your Loyalty?"

Let some of your Competitors continue to unintentionally appear insecure and self-focused by asking buyers for their loyalty.

Alternative Approach:

Thank buyers for their loyalty.

What's the difference?

Asking the buyer for loyalty is about you. Thanking the buyer in advance for their loyalty is about them, as in: "Folks, I just want to say that I appreciate your working with me among the 7,000 other Realtors® in this market and I want to remind you that, of course, due to our Code of Ethics (where applicable in your practice of Agency) you will be receiving my complete loyalty as we work together."

Transgression #5 – "Often times the First Offer is the Best Offer!"

Again, please don't point out the following to your competitors regarding how this Industry cliché can be interpreted by some Clients, such as asking:

• Can you show me the research regarding the statistics on this? Is it 12% or 87%, because this is too big a decision for us to rely on your limited anecdotal experiences.

• What testing construct did you use in your research?

• How would we know if this might be our best offer since we have no idea what might follow...and we can only go on your unscientific suggestion?

• I have a hunch that you are less likely to tell your Clients that, "Often times the First Offer is the Worst Offer!"

• Why don't you let me, the homeseller, judge the offer for what it is rather than nudge me to accept it? It seems as though you are actually more interested in getting my home sold than doing everything in your power to get me the best price! Yet, I read in the book *Freakonomics* that Real Estate Professionals wait longer to accept offers on their own personal homes.

When our Industry continues to champion this practice, of anecdotally announcing to homesellers that "The First Offer is often times the Best Offer," it might inadvertently stimulate more Consumers to believe, "If this is the case, maybe we should just try to sell our home ourselves!"

Alternative Approach:

During the "Marketing Proposal" explain, "Not only will I be presenting all offers, but let me also say now that sometimes the First Offer is the Best Offer and other times the First Offer is the Worst Offer. Because I represent you, I will help you interpret all offers based upon your circumstances and upon everything you have told me about your goals."

This way, when you believe the First Offer to very well be the Best Offer, you have built up prior credibility regarding this subject.

Transgression #6 – "I'm Going to Call the Listing Agent."

Do not interfere with this widespread practice either. If anybody in their right mind thinks that the term "Listing Agent" suggests "higher value," think again. Instead it conveys, "I have the listing, therefore, the biggest part of my job has been completed. It's listed!" Please do not interfere with this tsunami-like, horrific positioning.

Alternative Approach:

Rather, consider referring to that person (if they are a Realtor®) this way, "I'm going to call the Marketing Realtor®." Even saying they are a "Marketing Real-a-tor" (as opposed to a Realtor®) is a step up from "Listing Agent!" Although, don't expect to hear, any time soon, the words "Doc-o-tor" or "Archi-a-tect."

Transgression #7 – "It's Unbelievable!"

Whenever you overhear a competitor respond to the question, "How's the market?" with an answer such as, "It's unbelievable" (this answer is unbelievable), don't discourage them. No one likes a 'smart aleck!'

It's as if your Competitors believe this represents trusted, advisor-like deep knowledge or analytical brilliance. Or, if you hear them say, "All I need is a few more listings," as if the Consumer is going to reply with, "Why haven't you told us? Here's five!" Please don't meddle; just let your competitors continue underwhelming Consumers, causing them to think, "I guess I better change the conversation. Clearly, this person isn't comfortable discussing Real Estate since they responded with such a conversation-killing or room-clearing answer."

Alternative Approach:

You should say the following, "Thanks for asking. We are in a very opportunistic market. There are great opportunities for buyers, sellers, and investors...now let me ask you a question. When do you think you may be making your next Real Estate move?"

Transgression #8 – "I'm Serving Food at the Broker Open House!"

Hopefully someday, Real Estate Professionals will no longer need to enable gastronomic incinerator-like colleagues with the promise of a corresponding dining experience in order to seduce them into fulfilling their responsibility of becoming sufficiently knowledgeable of homes for sale in their market.

Illustration: Bertscha / Dalton / Ward

I just can't imagine somebody lying in a hospital bed and overhearing their doctor on the phone (the "Listing Doctor") asking another physician, "Will you please try to see my patient? I've ordered food for everybody... and, by the way, it's not hospital food. There's a great caterer in town I'm using!"

Of course, these Real Estate dining opportunities are confined to Industry members (through our roving version of an "employee cafeteria"), with very little dedication directed towards feeding Clients or Consumers as the rest of the world does!

Alternative Approach:

For example, here is what the automotive Industry advertises: "Come on down this weekend and bring your family. Look at our automobiles and enjoy the cook-out!" Perhaps we should be advertising, "Come join us at our company Open Houses this week and grab a snack while you're here!" Instead, our food budget never seems to extend to the Consumer, as we are consumed with culinary bribes to our colleagues in order to cajole them into becoming knowledgeable about what they have to sell. This is why when restaurants announce "Happy Hour" it is intended as a benefit for the Consumer and not fellow workers.

Transgression #9 – "I'm in Real Estate, but I Used to be a _____!"

Although only a small percentage of your competitors when asked, "What do you do for a living?" answer, "I'm in Real Estate, but I used to work for IBM" (as an example), don't point out why this might be deleterious to being considered a Real Estate Professional. Enough do this, however, that it is one of my 684 Real Estate things not to say.

Saying this is similar to someone announcing, "I would like you to meet my wife, Alice... and also say hello to my ex-wife Betty!"

When someone volunteers, "I'm in Real Estate but I *used* to be an engineer for Boeing," what they are really saying is, "Being in Real Estate isn't really 'who I am,' so can we change the subject."

<u>Alternative Approach:</u>

Repond: "Thanks for asking, I'm in Real Estate!"

Transgression #10 – "Here's How I am Different!"

When your competitors are asked by homesellers, "How they are different?" let them continue to fall into the trap of explaining how remarkable they are. As if homeowners are going to take notes, wake up their children, and invite their neighbors to hear about such greatness!

<u>Alternative Approach:</u>

Instead say this, "Folks, rather than focusing on how I'm different, I suggest we focus on how we have to have your home be appreciated for how it's different. I don't compete against other Realtors® in the marketplace as much as your home competes against other properties. I actually cooperate with the other Realtors®, but your home does not cooperate with other homes for sale. Therefore, the way that I am different is how we are going to show your Homes' distinctiveness."

For TownAdvisor Members reading this chapter, this is where you will add, "and not only does your home compete with other homes, but your town competes with other towns; which is why I have exclusively created a Town Website and Video. Let me show you the TownAdvisor Local Website, you'll love it." To which the homesellers will ask, "Who is going to see this Town Website and Video?" and the response is, "Every single buyer that comes through me."

To see example: www.TownAdvisor.com/WestportCT

Transgression #11 – "Recruiting and Retention is the Name of the Game."

While the military is consumed with "recruiting"... and prisons are relentlessly dedicated to "retention" ... Real Estate Leaders are in a league of their own in combining the two as an enduring tandem – e.g. "recruiting and retention." I respectfully suggest that our Industry consider substituting "recruiting" for "selection" and "retention" with "development."

Alternative Approach (example):

A leader who exemplifies this distinction is California Broker, Gino Blefari. Gino (my good friend), although a world-class CEO and operational wizard, for years met at 5:30 A.M. with "selected" Associates to personally conduct career developmental sessions. Due to Gino's dedication to development, clearly he never had a problem with "retention."

Transgression #12 – "The Buyer Determines the Price."

That there are still some of your competitors who actually think or say this should come as no surprise. For decades this stunning simplification of a comprehensive, multi-party-resolved transaction was offered up in Real Estate textbooks... and just passed on decade after decade without any challenge.

Here's the problem. If the buyer determines the price, why are you charging homesellers a hefty fee? This suggests that you clearly have no ability to determine any part of the outcome as a marketing, merchandising, networking, or negotiating pro.

Don't your competitors realize that banks (who are no different than the homeseller) also played a role in determining the final negotiated price?

Alternative Approach:

The buyer, buyer representative, seller, and seller representative all determine final price, along with the lender and appraiser.

It is also incorrect to say, "that the market determines the price," although it sounds good, and thus, is so hard to resist. In Real Estate (unlike stocks and bonds) the market does not determine the price. It only influences the price.

For example, you could be in the same market with the same property and the price that the home ends up selling for will be different each time you change any of the homesellers, buyers, and each Real Estate Representative for that one particular property. If this wasn't the case how could you ever make a convincing case (even to yourself) that you should be selected... if the market determines the price or the buyer? Otherwise, you are just facilitating something that you have no influence over, like someone who will sell your stocks or commodities.

Realtors® have far greater value than that which they are given credit for by Consumers, as well as that which they credit themselves.

Again, if you are representing a homeseller and you take on the assignment with the belief that the buyer alone determines the price that goes against the history of all retail, and all negotiating.

Thankfully, Real Estate is not one sided and there is a valuable role to play on each side of the transaction. Five different Realtors® might create five different pricing outcomes, even if there was only one buyer.

Transgression #13 – "I have a Listing Presentation tonight!"

If your competitors haven't figured out yet, here in 2015, that homesellers prefer "Marketing Proposals" over "Listing Presentations"... then stay out of this mess.

Alternative Approach:

Live in the world of creating and making "Marketing Proposals." Don't inform competitors that a "Listing Presentation" is about the agent and what they have done in the past. The "Marketing Proposal" is about the homeowners, the homes, and what is going to take place in the future.

Transgressions Intermission:
Before we move on to other clichés to avoid, please consider this...

It's not that your competitors (and perhaps, in some cases you) purposefully set out to alienate Consumers through ill-advised or insensitive communication, it's just that all of us (at times unknowingly) say things that create the opposite reaction of what we had hoped for... for example:

"No Problem!"

I am sure that the thousands of service workers who respond to a thank you from a customer with the words "no problem" actually would be surprised to know that their use of two negative words "no" and "problem" (as if asking for the check, or another glass of water, could ever represent a "problem averted") do not endear them to the customer. But this doesn't mean that you should point out to them, "How would you like it if you asked someone to marry you and they said, "no problem!"

Just as it is not your role to correct your competitors (for the reason aforementioned), I am sure that you have experienced an occasion when someone said something to you that offended you, and they could not understand why.

I know that I, on certain occasions after I have given a seminar have had very enthusiastic individuals approach me with the following message, "Allan, I liked some of what you said!" When this happens, I think, "I hope this person isn't saying to homesellers, 'I like some of your house!'" Whereas the top producers either say nothing... or they are profuse in their praise.

It reminds me of that old song, "You've got to accentuate the positive, eliminate the negative, latch on to the affirmative, and don't mess with Mister In-Between." Telling me that there were "certain things liked about the seminar", qualifies this person (as far as I am concerned) for the Mr. In-Between category!

An Insulting Contest

As a teenager I learned how important which words you select can be; especially when making points that pertain to a "sensitive" area. Unquestionably, people are extremely sensitive regarding any commentary concerning their homes

Speaking of sensitive subjects and the importance of using the right words, I recall how years ago while walking down the street with my two best friends how one said to the other right out of the blue:

"Tommy, it looks like you've put on some weight," Johnny exclaimed. To which Tommy replied, "I have Johnny! In fact, I've been meaning to tell you that I think your parents are a couple of pigs!" When Johnny went to physically attack Tommy I immediately had to break them up as I screamed at Tommy, "Why did you say that?" and I will never forget what he said: "Allan, I thought Johnny wanted to start an insulting contest...and I wanted to win!" Since Johnny hadn't seen Tommy in a year, he was surprised that this cyclist friend had put on weight. Yet later (after Johnny stormed off), Tommy said to me, "Allan, I don't like being called fat!"

Some people in our Industry also innocently say things like, "Let's take a look at the Comps," and do not realize how disheartening this can be for certain home-owners...to be told that other homes are "similar" or being compared to theirs.

As we move on to other examples of ill-advised Industry clichés, please keep in mind that 100% of your income is directly influenced by the words you choose.

End of Intermission

Transgression #14 – "My Negotiating Philosophy is: I Believe in Win/Win Outcomes!"

(So, why am i paying you to get me more?)

While this romantic notion might sound to some as a supportable premise, when some of your competitors voice this desired outcome as their stated mission, they overlook the following: It's called "Agency" where it applies.

Just as an owner of a professional sports team wouldn't hire a coach whose stated objective is "that all games end in a tie," if knowledgeable homesellers (or buyers) get a whiff of a Real Estate Professional whose major motivation is to "keep both sides happy," even though they (where it applies) only represent one side, this can be a cause for concern, if not consternation!

Some of your competitors will still try to justify this "Win/Win Philosophy" with the following rationalization: "Well, even if both sides cannot win, I do my best to try to at least have the other side 'think' they won! Otherwise, a transaction cannot come together."

This justification, however, does not change the fact that whenever you "fully" represent one side of a transaction (and there is not "Dual Agency" or you are not a Transaction Agent), then you should only be 100% dedicated and concerned with your Clients' outcome; even if you believe the other side ended up with a far less favorable and unhappy result.

I have asked the following question during seminars over the years: "How often have you observed a Real Estate Professional, when representing the other side of the transaction, reveal something about their Clients' circumstances that you believe they should not have?"

Based upon audience responses to the above question it might be accurate to describe this scenario as "representing an epidemic."

Do you think that psychiatrists, financial planners, and lawyers also routinely break Client confidences, or divulge sensitive information?

If your answer is "no" then you might agree that there may be a correlation between how a divorce attorney is less likely to tell their Client, "I am looking for a win/win outcome," than occurs in our Industry.

If someone is looking for a win/win outcome, then, of course, the thing to do would be to provide the other side with information that moderates your Client's goals.

Why are our Ethos (if not Ethics) different in the view of some? In my opinion, it is because most Realtors® repeatedly shift back and forth from being a Seller Representative to a Buyer Representative and this creates a schizophrenic-like career.

It would be the same as if an attorney four times a day switched from being a prosecutor to a defense attorney. This constant role-reversal may very well prevent such an attorney from ever fully developing all out representation or sympathies for one side of the law alone.

To the contrary, you can readily see how certain defense attorneys (when they appear on T.V. at least), always try to create the impression that no one is ever guilty. These professionals are always on the defense... which is why you'll never hear them say, "The middle rests its case!" No, it's always, "The defense now rests its case!"

Alternative Approach:

The only person who should ever be interested in a win/win outcome is a professional serving in the middle of two parties. This is the task of a mediator. Yet in most cases the Real Estate Professional has not been charged with the role of mediator. Regrettably some of your competitors overlook this distinction in what they divulge, in how they think, and in how they perform.

I think more can be done to provide Consumers with the sense that "all we care about is making them happy," even if it means having to conflict with other professionals whom we will be working with on future transactions.

Transgression #15 – "When would You like to Get Started?"

Whatever you do, don't correct this disaster! Since many homesellers either don't want to get started, or at best, have an approach/avoidance conflict on the subject, why would anyone ever ask this question? Rather ask them a question that pertains to what they want to happen. It goes like this...

Alternative Approach:

"How soon would you like to have your beautiful home sold to the right buyer?" Clearly, homesellers are more interested in having their home sold to the right buyer as opposed to "getting started." Keep this correction to yourself... you bought this book, they didn't!

Transgression #16 – "I have to Sit at an Open House this Weekend!"

If you ever hear a competitor say, "I have to sit at an Open House this weekend," again, do not correct them. If they don't realize at this stage of their career that this sounds one step up from saying, "I have to sleep at the Open House this weekend," don't wake them up!

Alternative Approach:

Say: "I'm marketing an Open House this weekend!"

Transgression #17 – "Do you Want Four Bedrooms?"

While I optimistically believe that the vast majority of your competitors are now emancipated from this early age Industry ploy "that you don't answer questions, just repeat the question," if there is anyone out there, in 2015, who is still a fan of this "just repeat everything that is said ploy"...let it go.

I remember when, during my first Real Estate training experience, our company's training manual informed us of the following: "When buyers call for information, don't give it to them. Instead, just repeat their questions so you get information from them instead."

To ensure that there was no misunderstanding, there were examples in our materials:

Caller: "Does the home have four bedrooms?"
Real Estate Professional: "Do you want four bedrooms?"
Caller: "Is there an echo here?"

Imagine if you went to buy a pizza and asked, "Do you have pepperoni pizza?" and the restaurant owner responded, "Do you want pepperoni pizza?"

Alternative Approach:

The alternative is quite simple... just answer the question!

This tactic, however, is consistent with how our Industry (at times) fights against what Consumers want when it is in conflict with self-interest.

To document this assertion ask yourself:

• What percentage of Consumers like Real Estate being displayed on the web... and IDX?

• Have we ever witnessed such fierce initial opposition to anything as our Industry's early battles to seek to prevent properties going online... and then, preventing Industry aggregation through IDX?

• Some of our chosen language is influenced by how most seminars are directed towards how Realtors® can become more successful as opposed to how Consumers can be better served... just take a look at any convention program and see if you agree. Now imagine if, at medical conferences, all of the workshops were devoted to how doctors can make better investments or reduce overhead versus focusing on medical solutions and treatments for patients.

Transgression #18 – "How are you Going to Select a Realtor®?"

Don't even think of correcting this beaut. What other professional on our planet would ever make this mistake?

Let me know the next time, when you are sitting face-to-face with a doctor, that the doctor actually turns to you and asks, "How are you going to choose a doctor?" Or, in other professions, when a landscaper, financial planner or a cleaning person brings up your process for selecting one of their contemporaries. Nobody, and I mean nobody other than Real Estate Professionals, voluntarily shoot themselves in the foot like this by bringing up competitors as potential choices.

Alternative Approach:

Instead you should ask, "Folks, what do you expect from your Realtor®?"

Think about it... a consultant would never ask, "How will you be picking a consultant?" as that displays competitive worry and who's to say that the prospective client is even interviewing others, so why introduce the topic? Instead, the consultant would ask, "What do you expect from a consultant?" and then move on to reveal that they can deliver on expectations. It's that simple!

The other problem with asking someone "How they are going to pick a Realtor®," is that it also suggests that we have to delay getting to homeseller concerns until we first resolve our pressing concern: "What process will you be utilizing to either pick me or my competitor?"

Ironically and tellingly, many homeowners weren't even thinking of entertaining choices; it's just that your competitors *compel* them to consider multiple options.

Realtor®: "How are you going to go about selecting a Realtor®?
Clients: I guess we shouldn't tell you... but we decided on you before you got here. Now that you brought this up though I guess we should interview others!

Transgression #19 – "Are you Aware your Home is No Longer on the Market?"

Why don't your competitors say, "Are you also aware that you had a car accident last week?"

For an <u>Alternative Approach</u>: see Chapter 5.

Transgression #20 – "Real Estate is a Commodity."

Any competitors who advance this notion completely undermine Realtor® Value, as well as display ignorance.

Why is it that a commodity trader would never say that what they sell (wheat, barley, copper, etc.) is "Real Estate", and stock brokers will never refer to the sale of IBM stock as "selling Real Estate", yet some in our Industry have actually and astonishingly dishonored Realtor® Value by claiming, "Real Estate is a commodity!"

Thank God this is demonstrably absurd. Why?

Someone at E*Trade will sell one million dollars of stock for less than ten dollars, and commodity trades also generate next to nothing in commissions.

Are you prepared to accept a seven dollar commission for marketing or selling a million dollar property? I assume not. Therefore, don't ever accept this concept that all Real Estate is "commonly priced" and "what you sell" are interchangeable widgets.

You never want to ask a homeseller, "If you owned stock and it was selling for one hundred dollars do you think you could ask for one hundred ten?" As you would never try this same, manipulative nonsense on a buyer by equally saying, "If a stock was selling for one hundred dollars, do you think you could offer ninety-five?" (When, in fact, you routinely encourage your buyers to offer less than the listed price.)

Your negotiating value as a Realtor® only exists in that financial outcomes in Real Estate are influenced by skillful representation on both sides of a transaction.

Homeseller Clients should never be given the sense that their negotiating opportunities are preempted by the powers inherent in the buying side of a transaction. Worse yet is when incorrect analogies are employed that seek to link how stocks and commodities are negotiated with Real Estate transactions. Rather, each and every Realtor® should be eternally thankful that Real Estate is not a stock or commodity for obvious reasons.

Alternative Approach:

Only that Real Estate is a sector (with millions of pricing nuances) and not a stock or a commodity that collectively rises and falls, often times one hundred times in the same day.

Transgression #21– "Homes don't Sell because of Price."

For an <u>Alternative Approach</u>, see Chapter 5.

Transgression #22 – "You've got to be Careful about Strangers Coming Into your Home!"

For an <u>Alternative Approach</u>, see Chapter 5.

Transgression #23 – "My Son plays Baseball Too!"

Many of your competitors confuse or conflate "identifying common denominators" with trying to one-up prospective clients.

For example:

Homeseller: "Our son just won a scholarship for baseball to Arizona State University!"
Your Competitor: "My uncle played baseball for the Pittsburgh Pirates!"
Mystified Homeseller: "We just got back from a trip to Italy."
"Let me top you" Competitor: "We went to Italy last year too... and we got to see the Pope. And then, from there, we spent a week in Paris!"

<u>Alternative Approach:</u>

Become part of their personalized joy!

Transgression #24 – "I've Received some Negative Reactions to Your Kitchen and the Fact that you Only have a One Car Garage!"

For some reason some of your competitors think that they are immune from the axioms "the bearer of bad news" and "shoot the messenger." My mother told me as a youngster, "Allan, you can say anything to anybody if you use the right *timing and tone*."

<u>Alternative Approach:</u>

"Folks, I've received some very positive reactions to your home (if true) but, unfortunately, due to today's buyer behavior in the market, nobody seems willing to pay over four hundred thousand for homes even as appealing as yours."

Transgression #25 – "We can Give it a Try at that Price!"

Given how almost all Real Estate Professionals overprice their personal residences, even though they have access to all the data, it helps to explain how many consumers imitate what Real Estate Professionals do when marketing their own private residences... they actually want to list their property higher than the data supports.

Therefore, if ever in your career you find yourself "taking" a listing at a higher price to start off with than you desire with the hope (over the next weeks or months) of getting a price reduction, at least don't destroy that opportunity (if it is your only or best opportunity "at that time") by saying what some of your competitors do, "Well, we can give it a try at that price and see what happens!"

This would be as confidence boosting as a fiancé saying to his future mate, "Well, we can try being married!"

Alternative Approach:

"Folks, we are shooting for a very ambitious result. I cannot guarantee that this desired price is achievable, but I will fight with every fiber of my being for that price as if this were my own home. That said, if we determine that we cannot generate the necessary responses at this price then we need to accept now that we will need to make an adjustment. Are you with me on this?"

Transgression #26 – "Can I get You to Sign In?"

When you bring your buyers to another Real Estate Professional's Open House and notice that "Marketing Realtors®" are still, in 2015, asking people to sign-in first, do not point out the counter-productive absurdity of this and the potential damage it causes your homeseller Clients.

Do not inform them of the following:

Basically, no one wants to sign-in and as a result of this annoyance they will:

• Write their name illegibly
• In some cases, lie
• Resent the home and Realtor® for having to endure this unique-to-Real-Estate security-related oppressiveness

Is there a better way to guarantee that no one will ever pick up a local homeseller Client (from the Open House) or cause buyers not to return than the absurdity of this practice? Unless, that is, you expect a call that goes like this:

"Yes! Hi, Susan. We were at the Open House on Sunday and, when we arrived, we didn't think that we were going to fall in love with the house, which we did when we saw the great room and the back of the property, so we lied when we wrote our names! We are really not the Smith's – we're the Lewis' – and we'd like to come back and talk to you about buying that home and listing our present home. I hope you are able to look past the fraud on our part, it is just that we were extremely uncomfortable at first."

<u>Alternative Approach:</u>

A better way, which I learned from Julie Vanderblue many years ago, goes like this:

Never ask visitors to sign-in when they first arrive. Just as Nordstrom's and Tiffany's (etc.) don't. Instead, ask permission from your homesellers to delay the request for when people are leaving the house and then get them to "sign-out." This comes after you've given buyers a reason for wanting to *have* you follow up with them... or after they've become monumentally more comfortable. Like everything else, you've got to earn their names... their correct names.

The way Julie does this is that she shows her Community Video for that town (on either a plasma, laptop, or tablet), asks for their opinion, and says she will be happy to email them the video's link or mail a DVD. They always give her their email, address, or both. It never fails.

In the meantime, please don't correct this century-old gambit employed by your competitors. No one likes to be told they are irritating valued consumers... especially over something so easily correctable.

By the way, Julie informs me that, almost without exception, all of her buyers now (very graciously and willingly) give their correct information when they leave and create a closer connection with her. The idea of delaying the request made of Open House visitors to sign-in (at first point of contact and until after greater rapport has been established), should also be considered in the context of safety as I outline in the bonus chapter at the end of the book, "Staying Safe...Professionally." Accordingly, one must decide the proper balance between safety and business success. While this is your personal decision, I encourage that safety must never be compromised.

Transgression #27 – "The Sincerest Compliment someone can Pay Me is to Send Me the Referrals of their Family and Friends."
(on back of business cards)

Alternative Approach:

"It would be my professional privilege to serve the Real Estate needs of your family and friends... referrals are deeply appreciated."

The difference? The first approach would be effective if consumers (not satisfied with just paying Real Estate fees) were seeking your direction, when not only trying to come up with a compliment for you... but rather a sincere one.

The alternative approach substitutes the concept of pleading for both compliments and referrals with a pledge and professional desire to serve a client's family and friends.

One method asks for their help, the other offers your help.

Transgression #28 – "When You're Ready to Buy or Sell a Home, Give Me a Call."

Alternative Approach:

"Contact me anytime for all your Real Estate needs or community information. Should you need to sell your home ... before you buy your next ... give me a call."

The first approach suggests: "You should only call me when I can make a sale. Until then you are on your own!"

Instead, you want to announce that you are always there for them. It is a simple yet important message.

Also, regarding "if you have to sell your home before your buy another" this addresses a major issue for millions of homeowners, specifically one that is completely under-addressed in Real Estate promotion. This announcement can lead to two transactions... both the sale, and then purchase, of Real Estate.

Transgression #29 – "The Reason you Should List with Me is...You Get Me!"

What many of your competitors may not realize is that to many homesellers this bravado represents the most frightening offer of the evening. This is because most people, including me, have to go well beyond just selling ourselves. Rather, we have to convince people of precisely what we are going to do and the value it will be to them – all of which, obviously, reflects upon us.

Now clearly you may think, "Well, that's what I mean when I say, 'You get me.'" But I want to make a distinction here. When most Professionals come into the Real Estate Business they are immediately told, "You've got to be able to sell yourself." Regrettably, many take this well-meaning advice literally... and without approaching this subject in a more nuanced fashion.

Alternative Approach:

Great salespeople that sell investments will sell the *merit* of the investments. Automobile salespeople are able to sell the *virtues* of the car. Technological and pharmaceutical salespeople draw strength from the *value* of the products and companies they represent. The great selling recruiters from Universities spend years on honing their skills regarding selling the *essence* of their institutions' and environments' to prospective student athletes.

Moreover, the most influential salespeople of all time become so because they sold something greater than themselves. For example, Roosevelt sold The New Deal, Truman The Fair Deal, Kennedy and L.B.J. The New Frontier and The Great Society, and (of course) Billy Graham is known for selling something bigger than all of the aforementioned put together... God!

Now clearly, the iconic contributors to this book are all able to proclaim to homeseller prospects the many benefits of selecting them. Yet, as you read their chapters (whether that be Russell Shaw and his "No Hassle Listing System," Jack Cotton and his world-class "Property Prospectus Program," or Julie Vanderblue and her handful of meticulously branded programs, as well as all of the other esteemed contributors to this book) you will find that they keep the focus on systems, programs, and services (albeit extensions of themselves) that are even more compelling than their considerable, yet finite personal value and charisma.

I have long wished that the Real Estate Industry would not continue to "leave out in the cold" so many Real Estate Professionals by essentially offering advice that suggests "That to be successful requires becoming a braggart."

Rather, the value of being a Realtor®, a CRS, a GRI, belonging to a great organization, the virtues of MLS and IDX, and an Industry networking paradigm (unlike anything in the history of organized behavior, when properly understood and leveraged) should make any Realtor® completely attractive.

I once read that, "When one is truly great you don't have to say it. Others will say it about you." As you read about the business practices of the legendary contributors who make up this book, you will see that all of them are able to lean upon not just who they are, but also, more specifically what they do... and what they each do is both different and distinctive. And, in respect of my personal limitations, this explains why I have asked a team of accomplished colleagues (beginning with Gee Dunsten) to write this book with me.

Chapter 2

Don't Just Differentiate...
Distinguish Yourself!

by Gee Dunsten
Past President of CRS and prominent Educator for the Real Estate Industry

Gee Dunsten:

Gee has been a senior instructor with the Council of Residential Specialists for almost 35 years and served as CRS president in 2001. Gee is president of Gee Dunsten Seminars, Inc. His hands-on approach to real estate training with leading edge ideas and systems has made him an in-demand speaker at NAR® conventions, and many state and company franchise conventions. Gee has taught in all 50 states, the Bahamas, Australia, Chile, and New Zealand...and has spoken on behalf of numerous Mortgage Companies. He currently teaches GRI courses and is the Director of Education for the online Certified Community Marketing Specialist designation. Gee has co-written and developed the Recreation and Resort Specialist (RRS) Training Courses and is recognized as a recreation and resort expert. Gee is a practicing Realtor® with Long and Foster Real Estate in Ocean City, MD and is credited with over 2,500 transactions in his storied Brokerage career.

Favorite Quote:

"In order to do something, you must first be something." – Goethe

Perhaps you have heard the expression, "That's a distinction without a difference."

Well, as a Realtor® I must say that for many years now I have heard my fellow Realtors® constantly exclaim, "How important it is to differentiate yourself in the market." Strangely, I never seem to hear, "You've got to either distinguish yourself or become more distinctive within your communities!" I wonder why?

One explanation might be that it's easier to figure out how we can be viewed as "being different" from one another (as there is so much emulation within our Industry) than in determining what is "required to be distinctive."

Now to ensure that I am being clear, permit me to reference the definitions of the words I am featuring here:

Differentiation – to make or become different
Distinctive – to be notable, attractive; possess special qualities

Actually, you want to both differentiate yourself professionally within your community, as well as represent distinctiveness.

If you have heard Allan Dalton speak, you might recall how he quotes the Dean of the Harvard Business School, "Businesses and business people must ask themselves two questions. First, What do I do that my competitors also do, but that I do better? That might be how you are distinctive. Secondly, What do I provide consumers that none of my competitors do? This is what makes you different."

I suggest that these two questions remain forever as part of all community business planning that you do; which Allan reviews in the last chapter.

Let me share what I've endeavored to do over my 30+ years of community-centric brokerage that has contributed to my producing 2,500+ transactions; leading to a similar number of satisfied clients. First, we must all understand that unlike many other businesses, where a remarkably distinctive product or service automatically offers differentiation, (to the contrary) we in Real Estate all get to sell the same product or inventory; homes on the MLS and IDX. Therefore we can't proclaim, "We sell Big Macs while they sell Whoppers" or "We sell a Mercedes 560 and they sell a BMW 750, yet our auto has this and theirs does not." We have to differentiate ourselves based more on "what we do" than on a "differentiated product." So, how does one differentiate oneself within the market, and in a way that is truly distinctive?

That must begin by you – as a community-centric Realtor® – determining what you need to do to be distinctive – not different – but distinctive within your community... which requires that you conduct a personal S.W.O.T. analysis (strengths, weaknesses, opportunities, and threats) for your marketplace.

Since one definition of distinctive is: "possessing special qualities," ask yourself, "What demonstrable special qualities do I need to develop (not just possess but develop) that makes me truly distinctive?" These are qualities that will enable you to do many of the same things that your competitors do, but also represent tasks that you perform (at a higher level of value) on behalf of your clients and community at large. This requires that you must make a personal commitment towards "learning our trade," versus merely settling for "learning the tricks of the trade."

As I stated earlier, my favorite quote is one attributed to the philosopher Goethe, "In order to do something, you must first be something." As we all know, there are no shortcuts to success in our business, and don't believe anybody who ever says that there are. Not one to ever seek shortcuts (for me) meant not just announcing, "I am a Realtor®," but completely, unabashedly, and relentlessly throwing my entire career at the altar of all that the National Association of Realtors® represents and offers.

Specifically, this meant attending all conferences, conventions, and enthusiastically participating in all educational, networking, and referral organizations that our Association provides us all with.

How can I possibly learn how to best serve my community (and its Real Estate needs) without also learning from others, who have already done so, admirably (for countless years), across North American communities?

We've all heard the axiom: "success leaves footprints." For me, that means: "footprints left on the beach."

What other Industry rivals the National Association of Realtors® in its willingness to generously share (albeit not always among local competitors) best practices? I can't even imagine a career that does not tap into such education and networking.

Becoming more distinctive within my community, by way of preparation (I will soon get to some of my specific methods of promoting my distinctiveness), also meant becoming a GRI and CRS (an educational and networking society which I went on to become past president of).

These three credentials (Yes, that's right. I said, "three!" First and foremost I am a Realtor®) provide me with pronounced distinctiveness within my community. I constantly call attention to these three credentials in all advertising, on my personal website, my TownAdvisor community website, and (of course) when I'm on marketing presentations.

For example, when I make a point about a certain marketing idea with a homeseller, I will always say, "One thing I learned as a CRS is that..." or "As a GRI, the first thing we are taught is...." I never and I mean never make a presentation without strategically inserting my professionally distinctive credentials into all discussions... but I do so subtly. For example, I don't stop all proceedings by declaring, "I am a GRI or CRS," as that would have lesser value to self-concerned prospective clients. I wait until I make an important point, one which I know the prospective clients will appreciate. Then I surround this point in the professional, credential-based way I mentioned.

I will also do this on every appointment now regarding my being a Certified Community Marketing Specialist℠ and I enthusiastically encourage you take this online course and become certified yourself. What homeseller in the world will not appreciate that you have learned and earned the right to be a designated Community Marketing Specialist℠?

"Becoming" before "doing" (as it pertains to distinctiveness), also means placing greater emphasis on the value of your "skills" even more than on the value of your "great service."

When the web first became prominent, many of my fellow Realtors® expressed concern as to whether their value would now be diminished. I guarantee you that engineers, doctors, lawyers (during that same time) were less fearful. Why? Because they view their role as being completely ensconced within the "skill sector." Too many Realtors® mistakenly see themselves as principally being "proud members of the service sector." Such mainstream positioning does not distinguish your high professional value within the local community.

Think about it! When you board an airplane, you will find two categories of airline employees: those who represent the "service sector" and those who represent "the skill sector." Whom do you want to be in the "skill sector," the pilot or the flight attendants? Need I say more?

Well, we are "the pilots of Real Estate transactions and beyond" and will never be viewed in this distinctive way if we first don't view our value at a higher level. While you want to represent both "excellent skills" and "outstanding service," you want to always be viewed as "a skilled professional who provides outstanding services" versus "a service person who also has skills."

This is why "being in the service sector" doesn't require designations in our industry.

Accordingly, as a "skilled professional," we must then manifest that we are knowledgeable regarding what the needs of one's community may be in Real Estate.

For example, if you've recently been working within a community, where there existed a preponderance of distressed properties, then clearly the way to become "distinctive" is to gain more knowledge; leading to a designation.
   (Please see our chapter or attend our course that covers this with Brandon Brittingham.)

If your market is resort and recreational dominant (as mine is in Ocean City), then that means becoming more distinctive (by elevating your knowledge here in this niche), again, leading to a distinctive designation: a RRS (which I also possess).

Remember, there might have been some time in your life where someone said, "Boy are you different," and it might not have been a compliment. Yet no one has ever taken offense when characterized as being "distinctive."

Jack Cotton, a legend in luxury marketing (featured in this book), has mastered the marketing of upscale properties. This is what makes Jack not so "different" as "distinctive."

Julie Vanderblue, a Fairfield County iconic Realtor®, is a true specialist in uniting her local business community to bring enhanced value along with her to her entire community (and is a proud member and leader within the Women's Council of Realtor® movement); all of which adds to Vanderblue's distinctiveness.

Jack O'Connor has distinguished himself as a true specialist in Luxury Golf communities.

The reason why I'm now offering a Certified Community Marketing Specialist℠ online course, which took our faculty a year to develop, leading to a Certified Community Marketing Specialist℠ designation), is to lead more of my fellow Realtors® to a higher level of strategic thought and implementation regarding their local success.

Allan Dalton's title for this book, *Creating Real Estate Connections*, says it all... it needs to be our number one objective!

Many of us live amongst enormous and untapped potential revenues within our local communities and, rather than powerfully inserting ourselves, we actually spend more time and money online waiting for buyers from the greater Universe; or, perhaps, the Twilight Zone.

Let me share some concepts that have truly made me "distinctive" in my market, and have created for me a world of Real Estate Connections.

Since I've been asked to list everything I've done in my career that speaks to distinctiveness, I've reluctantly listed the following:

1. **Marketing**
I've always had a fascination with marketing and I received my degree from the University of Maryland in marketing in 1969. I've was once called (by a brand president) a "Paradigm Breaker," and it's probably due to my insatiable drive to produce creative marketing solutions.

Over a 14-year period, I maintained top-of-mind awareness with my monthly targeted postcard campaign to current homeowners, past clients, out-of-town owners, and out-of-town agents. In the 80's and early 90's, I ritualistically mailed out over 4,000 postcards a month. Each card featured me, dressed up in that month's holiday costume; standing on the beach behind a "Sold" sign.

Examples:

   a) Easter Bunny – "Happy Easter!!!
The market is beginning to Hop
Whether you're thinking about
Buying or Selling,
We provide "Egg-cellent" service
Give "Me" a call so that we can
"get things hopping"
and Hurry, because the buyers
are multiplying.

   b) Hot Dog costume for
            Memorial Day
Just like our local Hot Dogs,
our business is "on a roll," too
        Especially when it comes to
            Buying and Selling Homes!

   c) Stork costume for Labor Day:
When it comes to marketing and selling homes,
we guarantee "Pain-free" Deliveries.

"Corny community comic relief creates lots of connections!"

My postcard campaigns garnered local, regional, and national attention, and led to recognition by the local and regional building industry. As a result, I created marketing campaigns for numerous builders/developers of single-family and condominium communities; which resulted in over 1500 transactions (this was the only way they could enjoy the marketing campaigns I made for them; by hiring me).

I will never forget the day when the largest developer in the area said to me, "Gee, we want you to make our properties Dunsten Distinctive."

2. Community

I've become known (within my local marketplace) as an innovator versus an imitator, and as a leader whom the community can turn to for results; someone who can overcome obstacles. While serving as a Commissioner for the Salisbury-Ocean City Wicomico Regional Airport, we were able to bring in our first major carrier, Piedmont Airlines; which now serves over 75,000-100,000 passengers flying in and out each year.

While serving on the Board of our local YMCA, we were able to raise enough funds to build a new facility with an indoor and outdoor pool (although, I prefer swimming in the ocean).

While serving on the Board of the Red Cross, we were able to develop a drown-proofing program that consisted of teaching water safety to elementary school 5th graders in a three-county area every year.

While serving on the Board of the Salisbury School, we raised enough funds to triple the size of the school. It went from teaching grades K-6 to teaching grades K-12.

3. Educator

My teaching career actually began while I was still in high school. At the time, I taught two to five-year-olds how to swim. I was also a Water and Safety instructor for the Red Cross, teaching the Lifeguard Certification course.

I'm known on a local and national level as the Real Estate Educator.

I've always had a thirst for knowledge. Early in my career, I taught Dale Carnegie courses in our local community; which assisted our local business leaders and their employees in improving their communication skills.

I was a faculty member at Salisbury University, teaching marketing to undergraduates.

I taught pre-licensing and GRI courses for the State of Maryland.

I've been a Senior CRS instructor for the last 25 years.

I'm president of Gee Dunsten Seminars, Inc. and have taught over 90,000 people in all 50 states, and as far away as Australia, Chile, and New Zealand over the course of my career.

I am a popular speaker at the NAR® conventions, as well as numerous state and local association conventions.

Locally, I am known as a coach, mentor, teacher, and trainer, which has fostered many relationships in and out of the Real Estate field.

I've also co-authored 3 Real Estate Certifications: Recreation and Resort Specialist (RRS), Military Residential Specialist (MilRES), and Short Sale Mastery (SSM), as well as a number of CRS classes for the Council of Residential Specialist (CRS). I'm very excited about our new certification course that we'll be rolling out soon called Certified Community Marketing Specialist^{SM} (CCMS^{SM}).

4) Top-producing Agent

I became a top-producing agent primarily as a result of the influence of two major icons in the industry, Howard Brinton and Allan Dalton (and as a result of the support of other industry leaders such as Del Bain, Rick DeLuca, LeRoy Houser, Pat Zaby, David Knox, Bill Barrett, and Dave Beson).

I was selected as a Star in Howard Brinton's Star of the Month Club and was featured in Star Power University.

I was inducted into the Real Estate Experts Hall of Fame in 2012 and was recently selected as one of the Top 10 Real Estate Elite Speakers.

I have always considered myself an educator first and a speaker second.

And now, let me end with my best idea; which represents the only endorsement I've made in my entire career (I have no financial interest in this company). If I had to trade everything I've done in my career, regarding community engagement, for this; I'd take this.

I (along with Town Advisor) created a local community third party website (www.TownAdvisor.com/OceanCityMD).

This was inevitable as, for years, I did a lot of business by making my personal website all about "greater Ocean City" and, when I used to share examples of this around the Industry in my classes, I would receive many "Wow"s.

I have evolved, though. Why? Because the web has also evolved and I needed not only to keep pace, but remain out in front.

I learned while attending an iBAR Camp that consumers like to go to specialty sites... and especially those where they can post comments. At this Industry-technology event, people were constantly talking about the relevance of 3rd party sites like Trip Advisor and Yelp. Therefore, when I heard about TownAdvisor, I was immediately interested, not only because it sounded like Trip Advisor and Home Advisor (not a bad thing), but also because TownAdvisor local community sites where engineered for consumer content; plus, the fact that the former CEO of Realtor.com viewed this as "where the Industry needed to go next," was also something I couldn't ignore. I also researched how consumers don't like feeling entrapped at so-called "gated sites." Therefore, as I looked at my own website (that provided community information), it occurred to me that my site could never be considered, by the community, as "its site."

So, I immediately reserved the TownAdvisor rights for Ocean City, MD. Beyond my Town-Advisor community website, the other major community initiative included in the program (and one that makes me dramatically distinctive) is my Real Estate Town Docu-Mentary[SM] Marketing System, and the Marketing System that accompany it. I'm the only Realtor® in Ocean City that's done a Real Estate Town Docu-Mentary[SM] and who has a marketing system to promote it (see my branded Flash Drive below).

The best thing (other than providing TownAdvisor with my suggestions about what's most distinctive about my town) is that I didn't have to lift a finger to have my community video and website created for me (at a fraction of what I thought it would cost, especially because it is exclusive). Now, I've become "the Talk of the Town" within Ocean City because of this production, and I mean the "Talk of the whole Town." What I love the most is how developers in the area assume I spent ten times of what I did to get these done.

Handing out Flash Drives of where people live... number one prospecting tool of my career. They love it!

In closing (and in keeping with the theme of *Creating Real Estate Connections*), the key to my greater success is not just in showing the community how I am distinctive, but demonstrate that I'm the best at capturing what is distinctive about where they call home; where they live. This how one "marketizes" an entire community; even before you break into niche marketing.

Dalton's Take-away:

It's very appropriate that one of our Industry's most distinctive professionals would speak to the subject of distinctiveness.

What makes Gee not only special and distinctive, is that he has devoted his entire career (beyond his prodigious personal brokerage) to educating much of the Industry. To his credit, Gee has done so without offending anyone that he has taught. I wish I could say the same for the rest of us, who seek to educate, coach and lead.

Chapter 3

<u>Creating Community Business Partners through Sharing Success</u>

by Julie Vanderblue

President of The Vanderblue Team –
Higgins Group - Christie's Affiliate

Exclusive TownAdvisor Member for
Fairfield, Westport, Weston, and Norwalk, Connecticut

Julie Vanderblue:

20 Year Top-Producing Realtor® with 80 - 100 Million annual production. President of The Vanderblue Team - a Higgins Group - Christie's International Real Estate Affiliate in Fairfield County CT, past President local chapter - Women's Couincil of Realtors®, Wall Street Journal honored Top 100 American Real Estate Teams. Top 10 Real Estate producer in the State of Connecticut. NAR® Convention presenter. Julie Vanderblue is legendary in Connecticut Real Estate circles for two things: Getting Homesellers top dollar for their homes and for the respect she commands from other Realtors®.

Favorite Quote:

"Nobody cares how much you know until they know how much you care." – Theodore Roosevelt

---

"Helping others become successful is the surest path to creating your own success." That was my belief, long before I realized it.

When I was in gymnastics, as a young girl, it was through coaching a child younger than myself that I became more passionate and, consequently, my own skill increased dramatically. It was after offering speeches to University students about "the importance of finding your WHY" that I thought to truly seek my own.

When I worked for Gannett, and became one of the top sales agents right out of college, it was NOT from selling full page ads to local businesses (as I was encouraged to do by management). It was through listening to business owners, then teaching them about strategic marketing, and creating long term plans. This is how I built a book of business which quickly surpassed my colleagues and competitors.

Being authentically excited about another's success, and then supporting them, is the most effective way to build loyalty, respect, and credibility.

Important note: This cannot be disingenuous or "performed" simply to win them over. In order to be effective, it MUST be from the heart.

Although my Team serves several distinct Real Estate Communities, my principal focus is Fairfield, Connecticut. I believe in this town. I love this town. I am part of this town. As the saying goes, "You can't sell what you don't believe in," yet this dubious approach is attempted by many, and it only leads to people feeling "sold."

Without question, when you believe in what you sell (or better yet are PART of what you represent), the notion of "selling" transforms into a consumer-enriching educational process. Consumers and clients recognize that you believe… and they want to believe as well. It is contagious.

Making the businesses in my community my "partners," to HELP them grow, is exactly what makes me grow…tenfold. Teaching my Team to do this in their own towns, and HELPING them become successful in their markets, not only bolsters the effectiveness of the Team at large, but it also significantly elevates my professionalism and success in turn.

Below are some examples of creative ways we support our community and, in turn, create more business and goodwill for our entire Team.

<u>The Vanderblue Neighborhood Network and Partnership Directory:</u>

This online and offline partnership directory not only incorporates the professional assistance that will be required to complete a successful Real Estate transaction (attorneys, mortgage brokers, inspectors, home service providers, etc.), but also includes our "Vanderblue Neighborhood Network." This network includes highly recommended places to dine, shop, visit, and patronize. Our partners truly appreciate being part of this and, because we are recognized in the community as leaders, it increases their own credibility when we regard them as partners.

> "When you believe in what you sell (or better yet are PART of what you represent), the notion of "selling" transforms into a consumer-enriching educational process. Consumers and clients recognize that you believe… and they want to believe as well. It is contagious."

<u>The Vanderblue 'Welcome to the Community' Gift Box:</u>

A favorite with our buyers (as well as buyers represented by others who purchase a Vanderblue property), is our carefully selected and subtly branded keepsake box brimming with gifts from our community partners. This is an extremely economical and strategic way for our chosen merchants to generate the first point of contact with these new customers that have just moved into town. It also makes them appreciate the Vanderblue Team every time a new customer comes to their place of business with our branded gift cards. They see that we are helping their business grow, and in turn, they send us their friends, families, and customers who are in need of Real Estate assistance.

This beautifully packaged gift is the first thing the new owner sees when they arrive at their new home. A lovely card (explaining that the local business owners are generously offering these gifts to welcome them to our tight-knit community) is accompanied by our booklet/partner directory of all participating partners. An example of some of the gift cards include: a bottle of wine, a half hour massage, 5 free shirt cleanings at the local dry cleaner, $50 toward a restaurant meal, half a cord of wood from a local landscaper (if they have a fireplace, of course), 1 free lawn care, free coffee and pastry, a small gift from a local shop, two free tickets to the local theater, a free haircut, etc.)

We do not charge our partners for this exposure, and they do not charge us for the card. If the card is used, we just brought them a new customer. If the card is not used, it cost them nothing and they gained exposure. The vendors LOVE this. Remember, the buyers have to go INTO the store to pick up these gifts, thus introducing them to this fine establishment. We do not allow percentages off (too tacky) but gifts at no charge. This adds up to thousands of dollars of free gifts and the new homeowners love it!

The Vanderblue Business Community Promotion:

The majority of our ads showcase one or more of our partners, in order to offer them visibly tangible support and recognition within the community: newspapers, The Vanderblue Property Guide, Blue Diamond Estate Guide, radio, high-quality magazines, internet ads, etc.

Many of our partners have told me that they believe our third-party endorsement carries more weight, within the community, than when they promote their business on their own. When they tell me this,I take this as an opportunity to remind them that when they promote me, it is even more effective than when I promote my Team. As business owners themselves, these partners welcome the concept that this can actually be a profit center for my Team, as well as free exposure by creating connectivity within the community.

Vanderblue Business Community Events:

We create and host multiple events each year, involving local small businesses. A community favorite is the "Vanderblue Holiday Gift Boutique Home Tour." Open to fellow Brokers and the community at large, this day of festive fun (where local merchants display and sell their products at our featured homes, and also offer slightly discounted gift cards for Holiday shopping to their local stores) is a fabulous way to increase the exposure of our homes, especially when the homes look so beautiful during the Holidays! The events support shopping in our own community stores, show people (not quite in the market to sell their home yet) that we are creative and they should consider us in the future, and allow us to get free exposure in the papers; as our local bank is the sponsor. Of course, we also buy Team gifts, stocking stuffers, and closing or Holiday gifts for our clients, to support our merchants. It truly is a win/win/win. Our homeowners, merchants, and the community all love this event!

The "Vanderblue Taste of Fairfield County Home Tour":

This event features a sampling of local eateries, provided free by our restaurateurs. We often select a reputable Mortgage Partner to sponsor this event, which enables us to advertise the logos of each restaurant in multiple ads. We also advertise this in New York (a market we try to capture), inviting them to come to dinner in Connecticut and sample the finest restaurants, while viewing beautiful homes. Each restaurant offers a gift card that we then raffle off to the attendees of our Open Houses. Again, a favorite!

The Real Estate Book:

In every Issue of the very reputable Real Estate Book, The Vanderblue Team is featured in the two-page centerspread and the "inside ad." This ad of our Team, surrounded by fine homes, also features one to four of our partners.

Previous examples:

"Get ready for Winter" was the headline and featured a local hardware store showcasing its generators, a gutter cleaner, a local plowing service, our partnering fuel company, a chimney sweep, etc. These partners pay to have their logo and contact information, and we create a helpful guide to the readers beyond just exposure to our homes.

Vanderblue Community Networking Events:

We have community networking events at local merchants' places of business. For example, a New Buyers Seminar at Las Vetas (our favorite coffee shop), a Guide to Investing in Real Estate at our Historical Museum (and they keep their shop open, as well as sell memberships), a Happy Hour in appreciation of our clients at one of our partnering restaurants, and educational seminar on short sales at a mortgage broker's location overlooking the water, a wine tasting to say "thank you" to our partner at our local liquor shop, etc. This is truly a great time to network, get to know our partners better, and show support by bringing new people into their place of business.

Halloween Safety Street:

My Team supports Halloween Safety Street, along with the local merchants. Rather than candy, we give out crayons and coloring books (designed and branded by us, of course), and hold a coloring contest with prizes from our local merchants (a candy store, ice cream shop, nail salon, batting cages, etc.) All of these are things kids love... and all local. This also gives me an opportunity to invite local families and children to my TownAdvisor site, and post comments in my "Neighbors Know Best^{SM}" and "Children Know Best^{SM}" sections, as well as post the winners of the contests on our Town Advisor site, our company website, our facebook page, and all of our social media.

Santa Comes to Town:

When Santa comes to Fairfield, he brings The Vanderblue Team along with him. A Mortgage Company sponsors this, provides Santa Hats for us, and we help the kids decorate them. We also get one of our partner's mascots (a great big Polar Bear) to come in costume and we sell tickets for pictures of the kids in their Santa hats with the cuddly bear. All proceeds go to our LOCAL Operation Hope, a homeless shelter and soup kitchen. It is a day of fun, recognition, and support.

We also send out photos of the kids (with the sponsor/Polar Bear) in our press released, and the supporters get more exposure.

Local Christmas Tree Lightings:

My Team also goes caroling at the Holiday Christmas Tree Lightings in several of our communities. Each is a night of bonding for our synergistic Team, in support of each community.

Vanderblue Community Coupon Days:

We also hand out Community Coupons at our open houses (on average 7-12 open houses per week) with offerings by our community partners. This again brings people into their stores and allows them to track where they are coming from, and they always appreciate that we support them. We are strategic with our partners about when and what we offer.

Examples:

- Buy One, Get One Free Lunch – get to know the restaurants while checking out Fairfield

- 20% off Potted Spring Flowers at our local garden shop during Mother's Day

- Two for One Pinkberry on a summer afternoon

- 20% off from a local jewelry store the week before Valentine's Day

- Free Wreath, when you cut your own Christmas Tree at Maplewoods Farm

Luxury Home Fundraisers:

We offer our luxury homes (with the blessing of the home owners) as venues for MAJOR local fundraisers. We have raised upward of $25,000 and created great awareness and goodwill (not only for our homes but within our community). Our Community Merchants offer many of the auction items that raise this money, and they get incredible exposure (both in advertising and at the event). Goodwill for all!

Vanderblue Team Open Monday Meetings:

We invite our business owners to join us at one of our meetings EVERY Monday (they usually insist upon providing breakfast, which is great for us!) They educate us for 15 minutes about what they do, and how they can help our Team grow. This creates face-to-face valued relationships with our Team and often the education helps the agents grow.

We also find that we get more referrals for buyers and sellers from these partners, after they come in and meet with the whole Team.

Vanderblue Nights of Gratitude:

We have yearly partner appreciation parties, a Vanderblue Night of Gratitude. This past year, we played our Real Estate Town Docu-Mentary^{SM}, and it received a thunderous ovation. It was such a hit that many asked for branded copies of their own, to distribute to show their support, belief and pride in the town. We buy the food, drinks, and party gifts from our partners and our local town glossy magazine supports the event with a gift to all in attendance (giving them exposure to these businesses).

The Vanderblue Community Website:

Until this year, I had always simply added information about many towns on my personal website. After all, buyers want choices, and it's important (that when buyers are looking for a buyer's agent) that they immediately recognize that I possess deep knowledge and impartiality regarding all Fairfield County Towns.

When I am looking to attract homesellers, however, it is the opposite. Homeseller clients want, and expect, me to point out what is distinctive and even better... about both their home and town.

I couldn't play "town favorites" on my personal website and, since I had to treat all towns the same there, this didn't give me a competitive edge with, or for, town homeowners.

Now I have the best of both worlds.

I can cover information about all towns on my personal website (which is the right thing to do for all buyers) but, with my exclusive Fairfield TownAdvisor.com website, I can appropriately (before representing any one buyer) and completely promote all of the virtues of Fairfield and other towns individually.

This also gives me the opportunity to prospect to local homesellers, both to ask them to contribute posts on how they like living in town, and to encourage town homeowners to come to "their" town website (which I host) to check out what it says about living where they do.

Obviously, this is different than telling the town to, "Check out my personal site!" It is asking them to, "Celebrate their own Town Site!"

Also, on my TownAdvisor local Town Site, the MOST impressive and cherished gift my Team and I can offer our community, is our Real Estate Town Docu-Mentary℠ – which tells the story of the town like no other. The entire community falls in love with the "picture we paint" about the town we serve.

At the end of the day my overarching strategy, regarding coordinating local merchants (in an effort to attract more customers to their businesses) is to increase the likelihood that these buyers will value our community more and, therefore, be willing to pay more (unless they are my buyer client, of course) for the privilege to live in each

town I showcase through my community websites and videos.

51

The more that all buyers value our towns, the stronger our home values will be. Sophisticated homesellers appreciate this Vanderblue Team strategy.

As I write this, I want to offer a cautionary note before anyone implements these ideas I have outlined. Beware! You may become an embarrassment to your children. You will see what I mean.

Just a few hours before I sat down to write this, my daughter hesitated when I asked her to come to the store with me. My feelings were hurt a bit, so I asked, "Greta are you getting too old to spend time with me? Do I embarrass you?" She laughed and said, "No, Mom, it's just that every store we go into, everyone knows you, and we stay too long."

"What are you talking about? That's not true," I replied.

"Mom, when is the last time we walked down the street and at least two people didn't stop you to talk. Or when we go to 'just pick something up' you chat with the owner forever (dramatizing, 'foorreevvver!') It's like you're the mayor or something. I have homework, and I just don't have time for that!"

I smiled and promised I would be mindful of her time. She smiled back and said, "Actually, Mom, it's kinda cool."

My heart grew three sizes.

I thought to myself, someday she'll understand that these relationships within our community are going to help me pay for her college tuition.

My partners know that their success is important to me and, in turn, my success is important to them. They have families. They have friends. They have customers and they refer me. Not because they feel they "owe me" or feel that they "have to in order to get my business." They do this because they trust me. Because they like me. Because I am "family." It's that simple.

When I was invited by Allan and Gee to contribute to *Creating Real Estate Connections*, I was asked to limit my community-based idea sharing to essentially "what I do to network and connect among my community businesses." The reason I point this out is that this is just one element (although a very important one) of my overall business. I also didn't take the time to include all of the charity work and civic participation that all members of our Team are noted for within all of our communities. For as committed as I am to the communities where I work and reside, it can never compare to the obligation I have to serve my clients.

Most of my clients are homesellers, as my specialty is on the marketing side of our profession, since this skill set correlates to my entire background.

So to be clear, "the niche" that I have focused on for this book is one that, perhaps, you can do more of... and can help you enjoy greater success.

Just as I look forward to carefully reading all other chapters within this book (so I can learn other methods of strengthening my Real Estate connections), please feel free to contact me if you ever want to discuss any of the above ideas, or if I can help your career in any way. As I mentioned at the start, it's through supporting others that I become all that I can be.

Dalton's Take-Away:

If you are playing Real Estate checkers then Julie has identified a marketplace segment ... community merchants.

Julie however is playing Real Estate Chess... as she is "desegmenting" her market.

Julie realizes that, through local merchants, she reaches a broader market – one composed of all niche markets... and especially all homeowners.

Better yet, within this segmented market, the merchants are honored to pay for her advertising costs so they can both reach the larger desegmented market... a win/win all around!

If you are being coached *(and plan to implement strategies from this book)*, I suggest before doing so you review each and any idea you are considering with your coach... to see how and where they may fit into your overall business strategy.

Respectfully,
Allan Dalton

Chapter 4

How to Become a Luxury Market Leader
an interview with Jack Cotton
Real Estate professionalism personified

by Gee Dunsten

Jack Cotton:

Jack Cotton with Sotheby's International Realty Osterville Brokerage has worked continually in the real estate business he started in his college dormitory room in 1974. Over three decades, Cotton Real Estate became one of the most admired and professional real estate companies on Cape Cod.

In 2005, Jack sold his company to Sotheby's International Realty. He transitioned away from sales to growing, running and managing the firm's Cape Cod offices while working with selected clients.

In the fall of 2008, he stepped down as the manager and has recently returned to being an agent.

Claim to Fame: Jack has been involved in nearly every record breaking luxury residential sale on Cape Cod, either directly as the agent or as coach to the agent involved. Jack likes to write in his spare time. His first book, "A Dog's Guide to Life" is in its second printing. "Selling Luxury Homes" and the "12 Secrets Luxury Home Buyers Know" were published in 2010. "12 Secrets Luxury Home Sellers Know" was published in 2011.

Favorite Quote:

"The doors of wisdom are never shut." – Benjamin Franklin

Gee Dunsten:

Jack, how did you get into the Real Estate business?

Jack Cotton:

Having grown up in Cape Cod with a single mother and two sisters, it seemed there were always lots of people around. I enjoyed building treehouses and forts, which provided a safe oasis from everything that was going on around me. In those early days, the Cape wasn't as developed as it is today, so there was always an abundance of lumber for me to use. My love of treehouses, homes, and Real Estate, continued throughout high school and college. While attending college, I finally made the decision to go after the Real Estate business as my career. No classes were being offered in Real Estate in college, so I took finance and business classes to help me prepare. I actually launched my career in Real Estate in my dorm room, but my first official office was located in a corner of my Dad's plumbing warehouse. There was only one phone which I shared with the plumbing business, so when it would ring we were never sure if it was going to be for plumbing or Real Estate.

After graduating at 21 (but only looking like I was 15), and with no real experience in Real Estate, I determined the best opportunity for me existed in property evaluation. There was no such thing as CMAs at the time. Most agents didn't do much, if any, research. They basically walked around the house building rapport and "feeling the seller out" about what they wanted, and then gave them a number. There was very little specific data to support their pricing recommendation, as well. Most homeowners were influenced by their gray hair and nice clothing. I knew that I could do a much better job, so I decided to read every book I could find on the subject of appraisals and take every appraisal class available.

G. Dunsten:
So what did you do differently?

J. Cotton:
I started doing detailed narratives of 30-40 pages (regardless of price) with facts about the area, floor plans, charts, graphs, photos, statistics, cost per square foot, details about the market, as well as specific examples of homes for sale and those that sold. I included anything that would be relevant to eliminate the guesswork in determining fair market value. I realized that the more information and data that I provided, the more creditable I became; in spite of my age.

G. Dunsten:
What launched your entry into the luxury market, Jack?

J. Cotton:
Gee, it was when I met my "maverick," that one person who was not afraid to go against the grain and take a chance on me. She was an elderly widow, whose husband had been a very successful attorney with a very large and prominent law firm, and who (on the advice of a friend) requested an evaluation. This evaluation was on not only one, but two properties she owned. It turned out that one was a home worth $90,000 and the other was a residence worth $200,000. Keep in mind that, in those days, an MBA from Harvard was only making $15,000, therefore, both of these homes were considered very high end. Today, that $90,000 home is worth $2.5 million and the $200,000 home is on the market for a little under $6 million.

G. Dunsten:
Once the door opened for you, how did you establish yourself in the luxury home market?

J. Cotton:
When working in a wealthy community, you must create what I refer to as: "an aura of expertise." The wealthy crave expertise and knowledge. Similar to going to their doctor or dentist for an annual checkup, they also require yearly updates or assessments

of their assets and investments for tax purposes, financial planning, trusts, and more. Accordingly, they have a number of professionals, such as lawyers, CPAs, estate planners, financial advisors, etc., whom they frequently rely on for guidance. I discovered that often, when it came to Real Estate evaluations, most of the information was limited and in the form of a mere appraisal, which often fell short of expectations. By providing a 30-40 page narrative for their clients, we afforded the various financial professionals, the opportunity to more confidently make recommendations to their clients. Moreover, because we always provided the same amount of effort and detail of analysis for every property regardless of price, word began to spread from one financial planner to another to not only use us, but to encourage their clients to use us for their annual real estate checkup. In other words, one widow led to another."

One of my biggest sales was $19 million. 100% of that transaction came from our yearly property evaluations for a widow in our community for tax and trust purposes, etc. As I've said before, I've always done the same amount of work for everyone, from the $19 million home to the $149K home I have evaluated this year.

G. Dunsten:
Jack, why are there so few agents working the high-end market?

J. Cotton:
Most Real Estate agents are afraid or intimidated to enter the luxury market for fear of being asked how many homes they have sold in the client's community. In reality, there is no discrimination in this segment of the market. In the wealthy community, when it comes to Real Estate outcomes, there are fewer problems with race, heritage, religion, politics, or sexual orientation. Wealthy people only want two things:
  1. Results
  2. Expertise

Recently, I had the opportunity to interview for a listing in an affluent community where I had limited exposure, not having been involved in any transactions in that community. One of the first questions the homeowner asked me was, "How familiar are you with the community and how many homes have you sold here?" Because honesty is always the best policy, I told him that I had not sold anything in the area, but I had a proven track record in high-end sales of homes in other similar communities on the Cape. Sensing further reluctance on the part of the seller, I told him that, "I pledge to commit to a 100% focus on your property and not to work with other properties in your area until your home is under contract." How often does someone commit to 100% of their time and energy focused on their property until it sells? It might only work half the time, but that's 50% more than those who are afraid to show up.

G. Dunsten:

How complicated is working with wealthy clients?

J. Cotton:

The self-made wealthy are the easiest to work with. They see a little of themselves in you and are excited to help you make your mark with their property. Nothing works better in the luxury community than when creating a bond based upon mutual respect or effectiveness. They have the same dreams, designs, and levels of achievement, and quite naturally gravitate to other professionals who manifest these same revered qualities.

G. Dunsten:

Jack, what suggestions do you have for increasing your visibility in the luxury market?

J. Cotton:

Gee, wealthy clients have three things in common and they intersect in the middle.

You must work with these three communities:

1. Those with great wealth - Marketing to the wealthy community is easy to do. All wealthy people are involved in their high-end community. They are activists. You have to think like you are wealthy. They have pride in where they live and are concerned about preserving their quality benefits of living there, while keeping property taxes low.

   a) I strongly recommend that you join the same service clubs and organizations they belong to (some you won't be able to get into), such as Non-profits, Charities, Historical Society, Places of Worship, Environmental issues/concerns

   b) Volunteer and take an active role in places where you can be seen, such as: Library auctions, School bazaar, Hospital fundraisers, Local talent shows, etc.

2. Their gatekeepers – You must also market to their gatekeepers, the financial planners they see for their annual checkup. They will need someone like you to contact for their client's update on Real Estate. The wealthy will need to add a Realtor® to the update list.

   a) Attorney

   b) CPA

   c) Estate Planner

   d) Trust Officer

   e) Insurance Agent

   f) Retirement Planner

3) Their service providers - You will also want to market to the service providers of the wealthy. They have your future clients on direct dial and it's usually their cell phone number!

- a) Yacht Club employee who works on their radar/technology/equipment
- b) Golf Club Pro –
(the guy who replaces their grips)
- c) Tennis Pros –
(lessons pro & person who restrings their racket)
- d) Personal trainer or fitness coach
- e) Pool maintenance guy
- f) Yard guy/landscaper
- g) "Bat-proof your house" guy – (My wife hired one who had a billionaire on speed dial.)
- h) Local florists
- i) Interior designer
- j) Appliance repairman
- k) Exterminator
- l) Party planner
- m) Caterer
- n) Wedding planner
- o) Professional photographer
- p) Local computer repair guy
- q) Contractor/remodeler
- r) Wine/liquor store
- s) Hardware store
- t) Butcher shop

Jack Cotton:
Real Estate Professionalism Personified.

I'll share with you an idea I got from the renowned restaurant, Anthony's Pier 4 in Boston. When the restaurant was newly-opened and looking to establish itself as a top-end eatery, the owner invited taxicab drivers from all over the city to come for a free Porterhouse steak dinner, offering them a steak so big it falls off your plate. It generated so much positive, word-of-mouth feedback that the owner continued to do it year after year. So based upon the success of Anthony's Pier 4, I decided, once or twice a year, to invite the service providers in my area to dinner and a free, mini seminar about how to do low-cost/high-impact marketing. I tell them, "I will help you grow your business and you will help me grow mine."

G. Dunsten:
Do you have any other tips for success, Jack?

J. Cotton:

You must provide the highest level of service in the following five areas:

1. Markets and evaluations (macro) – (overall market – demographics, economics, cost/sq. ft.)
2. Pricing (micro)
3. Market preparation (staging) experts
4. Marketing
5. Negotiation

Wealthy people are gluttons for information and are not choosy about the source. They will ask anyone and everyone to help them sort through and select what seems to be the most reliable and credible information. They are ravenous consumers of information. As agents, we should be not only the source of the source of information, but also the interpreter of the information, so we can provide the best advice with confidence, regardless of their social standing and professional success.

Dalton's Take-away:

I emphatically encourage you to get a copy of Jack's book, Selling Luxury Real Estate. Even though the pedigree of Jack's brand, Sotheby's International Real Estate, is synonymous with the ultimate in quality... the brand name "Jack Cotton" seems to be accomplishing the near impossible: it's actually making the Sotheby's International brand even more remarkable and illustrious within Jack's elite Cape Cod communities.

When somebody covers a subject that they have mastered, in such a masterful fashion, there really is nothing left to say... but, since that's never prevented me in the past, let me add this one last personal tidbit.

You may want to use this as your ice-breaker with all of those with grandiose properties. It goes like this, "Folks, I'd like you to know I feel extremely comfortable and at home visiting your exquisite and compelling residence, because I grew up in a similar sized property myself... although, I must acknowledge, there were six other families living with us in the building."

Chapter 5

Fighting For (not Against) For Sale By Owners and Expired Listing Homesellers!
(Scripts Included)

by Allan Dalton,
Co-founder, TownAdvisor.com & Former CEO of Realtor.com

In keeping with my theme of "fighting for" versus "fighting against" community members, I feel compelled to convey the following: The Real Estate Industry has been 'fighting' against "For Sale By Owners" for decades and these homeselling-related hostilities do not appear to be lessening; especially given our current Industry paradigm regarding For Sale By Owner communication.

Here are my "bullet points" (forgive the pun) which I believe validate my dramatic assertion that leads many For Sale By Owners to conclude we are "fighting against them"... and certainly not "for them:"

1. War time adversaries, or sociological threats, are routinely dehumanized or demonized through the use of abbreviated slurs. Yet you will notice that the victims themselves do not refer to themselves in the same fashion. Whereas people referred to as doctors also call themselves doctors, Americans call themselves Americans, FSBOs and Expireds (with good reason) break from that tradition.

Trust me, For Sale By Owners do not refer to themselves as "FSBOs." Homesellers whose property did not sell do not ask their neighbors, "Are you a fellow Expired, too?" Regarding the relentless use of the word "Expireds," one has to wonder (when non-industry people hear this expression) does this suggest that a Real Estate Professional is heading over to their local cemetery (shovel in hand) for a night of moonlit-aided grave digging?

Such slurs, however, make it easier to dismiss human beings as individuals and valued members of our community through unfair and disrespectful collective labeling.

One abbreviated word can also, perhaps unwittingly, abbreviate dignity, respect, and all hope for compassion, understanding... and, in the case of For Sale By Owners, for mutually respectful engagement.

2. The Industry favored question: "Have you had many offers?"

This is like going into a restaurant where no one is eating and asking the owner:

Illustration: Ward/Dalton

Also, take note of the way the question is normally posed, "Have you had many offers?" versus "Have you had *an* offer?" This is because the question "Have you had an offer?" does not offer as much potential to humiliate those some are fighting against.

3. Actually telling a For Sale By Owner: "You have to be careful about strangers!"

What do you think you are? Also, do you really think that homeowners view this "warning" as a way to reflect a deep concern for their family's safety... or rather as a desperate, fear-mongering attempt to get a "listing?" Moreover, I remember reading once that over 90% of the violence in homes is initiated by loved ones or family members. Therefore, ironically, homeowners are statistically safer with visits from strangers.

4. Telling homeowners that, "FSBOs net 10% less than when represented."

This is a completely unprovable statistic (as one can never project what a home would have sold for under a different approach) but, here again, this is where we come across as fighting with homesellers... always anxious to prove them wrong!

5. "You cannot qualify buyers."

Realtors® do not qualify buyers... lenders do... and homesellers have access to lenders too.

Why such desperate and disrespectful approaches to these important members of our community? As if antagonizing prospective homeseller clients would, in any time or place, be an effective strategy!

Here's why:

It all begins with our Industry conveniently conflating the words "sell" and "market."

When it is not clearly appreciated that when working with or representing homesellers "we market" and when working with or for homebuyers "we are selling"... which leads to actually believing that we and For Sale By Owners are both trying to "sell homes."

The belief that we "sell" versus "market" homes (unless also involved in dual agency), when on the homeseller side of the transaction, forces natural competition between Real Estate Professionals and homeseller aspirations to arise. Consequently, War breaks out for we are both trying to sell the same product... therefore, there is a natural and inherent competition over who can perform this task better.

Competition can be a synonym for fighting and fighting can, at times, be viewed as War. Thus, this explains why these community members must be reduced to war-like expressions, such as "FSBOs."

Based upon The Principle of Reciprocity, all of our thinly veiled fighting words (as just referenced), dedicated to telling the For Sale By Owner homeseller what they cannot do compels homesellers to search for equally disqualifying reasons to not use you and your services. They must respond in kind... by pointing out what YOU can't do.

Here is a more community-respectful way to better embrace For Sale By Owners as respected members of the community and dramatically increase effectiveness.

For Sale By Owner Suggested Script:

Real Estate Professional: "Folks, if all you want to do is 'sell' your home you do not need me... because you can clearly sell your own home."

Explanation:
- This language is true.
- This language is disarming because it is unexpected and respectful.
- This language moderates the benefits of selling by the use of "if all you want to do."

Real Estate Professional: "But, if you would like to 'market' your home, I would love to represent you!"

Explanation:
- This language displays your skills and knowledge and educates homesellers that there is a difference between selling a home and marketing a home.
- By first acknowledging they can sell (due to the same Principle of Reciprocity), they are now willing to acknowledge that *you* can market. Both sides keep dignity... the fight is over.

Real Estate Professional: "When you sell a home, you sell to a buyer... when I market your home, I 'have it sold' to the 'right buyer'. I don't want to 'sell your home'... I want to 'market it' because all pricing is governed by the laws of supply and demand... and I want to maximize the demand!"

Explanation:
- Now that you have "tenderized" the homeseller and put an end to the fighting, you can then introduce more intense points... such as how both they and the buyer cannot save the same commission. Corporate relocation buyers are not sitting in hotel rooms circling For Sale By Owner ads, etc.

- These ratcheted-up points can now be made, as the consumer respect displayed dissolves defensiveness and envelops you and the homeowner(s) in a loftier and more professional premise and goal: Marketing.

Now that the fight is over and mutual respect has been established, then and only then, can true communication take place.

One last point... perhaps if our Industry (in an act of "Industry self-respect") would stop referring to those representing homesellers as "the listing agent" (a description that suggests that all one does is "list" and therefore one's ultimate accomplishment has already been satisfied) and instead used the following attribution in its place: "Who is the Marketing Realtor®?" (when a Realtor® is representing the homeseller). Then more consumers would better appreciate the difference between "marketing a home" versus merely "listing a home."

Clearly, homesellers can perform both listing and selling duties, but few, if any, can rival our world-class marketing – a seminal point that remains under-appreciated throughout an industry still rejoicing in the word "listing" and where listings (and not marketing) is the name of the game.

This means that all the Homes Guides (with little boxes with the invitation "Your Listing Here!") would have to be changed to "Your Home Featured Here!" ... a shift that pays greater respect and better connects us to our communities.

Expired Listing Overview and Scripts

Let us now examine how we can more robustly and respectfully "connect" with those homesellers whose homes have not as yet sold (so labeled "Expireds") and community homesellers who are in need of a marketing upgrade.

As any psychology course primer would readily posit: "When one does not respect oneself, it becomes difficult to show respect to others."

At first glance my oblique assertion (that our Industry does not fully respect the value we provide homesellers) might be greeted with scorn. Well, since I too wish to connect with you instead of alienating you, let me see if I am able to defend this statement while at the same time connect my explanation to how North American homeowners are engaged when their home is not sold during the marketing agreement time-frame.

Here goes:
In the 1950s the corporate world was introduced to the concept of "The Four P's of Marketing: Pricing, Packaging, Promotion, and Placement."

This revelation (one offering stunning clarity in the "successful" marketing and selling of all products) enjoyed widespread acceptance. Unfortunately, not so within the Real Estate Industry. As if what we sell, "highly distinctive and customized lifestyles," is not as deserving of such comprehensiveness as "interchangeable widgets."

Our Industry instead instantaneously rebuked three-fourths of this Circle of Success claiming: The only "P" that was relevant in the Real Estate Industry was the "P" that stood for Pricing. Consequently, the following collective mind-set continues to evolve to this day: "Hey, you could have five dead bodies in the basement of the home for sale... but if you lower the price enough it will still sell!"

Wow, what an indictment of our marketing power and such a blow to the Industry's self-respect; not to mention the higher value we wish to represent and be respected for.

To the point that maybe a home didn't sell due to the other "P"s – Product (staging), Placement (advertising, enhancements on the web, etc.), Positioning (networking, competitive description of property)... there was a one P (pricing) Industry-convenient response here as well: "Even if there is no staging, no advertising, no networking, and horrible negotiating... if you lower the price enough (code word: "priced to sell") someone will buy it."

By discarding 75% of universally accepted practices and principles of what is required to successfully market a product (all Four P's) and instead defaulting to merely one "P" (Price... with the objective of merely creating a sale), it resulted in the following:

1. Our Industry's growth, and thus self-respect, was stultified (as if the only reason a home didn't sell was due to price... then, conversely, the only reason a home did sell was due to price). This minimalistic approach subliminally suggests that Real Estate Professionals were merely overpaid appraisers versus world-class marketers and this is an unfortunate notion, as many in our Industry (while not – as yet – are as proficient in marketing entire towns and cities as part of their overall lifestyle marketing responsibilities), are truly quite accomplished at marketing individual homes.

2. Our Industry, by over-focusing on just the "one P" (price) versus equally embracing the other three, led to an under-appreciation of the marketing Realtors® do. I witnessed this myself while CEO of Realtor.com.

Expectedly, if you are repeatedly reminding yourself that the "only reason" or "the major reason" a home is not selling is the price (to almost Gregorian chant-like observance levels), then clearly this is not a motivation to do more Merchandising, Marketing, Networking, and Negotiating on behalf of the homeseller.

Alternative Thinking and Approach:

There is only one reason for a home not selling: MARKETING... because, while Price is part of Marketing (one of the Four P's), Marketing is not part of Price.

This career-enriching appreciation completely changes how one feels towards and communicates with so-called "expired-listing" homeowners.
Now, let's review the language that Expired listing homesellers will embrace and positively respond to.

Expired Listing Homeseller Suggested Script

Real Estate Professional: "Hello _____. I see, according to my MLS information, that we are no longer able to sell your home and I would like to know if you would still like to have your home sold?"

68

Explanation:

• Do not say, "I see that your home is no longer on the market." Just because it is off MLS does not necessarily mean they consider it "off the market," so why fight over this point?

• It is hard for earnest homesellers to admit that they do not want their home sold.

Real Estate Professional: "I specialize in representing homeowners whose homes haven't sold yet... that I believe should sell."

Explanation:

• A lot better than, "I represent homeowners whose homes have not sold... and which I think will never sell!" Only kidding!

• Don't ever say, "Are you aware that your home is no longer on the market?" unless you think the "bearer of bad news" and "shoot the messenger" expressions exempts our Industry. Why don't you also call homeowners, interrupt their peaceful evening, and tell them, "Are you aware your son flunked chemistry?" or "I heard you lost your job!"

Real Estate Professional: "Has anyone told you 'why' your home did not sell?"

Explanation:

• If they answer "no" you should say, "There is only one reason why homes do not sell... it's due to the marketing." Now that you understand that Price is part of Marketing you can resoundingly make this hopeful and optimistic point to beleaguered homesellers and not feel you are being disingenuous.

• By announcing that "Marketing" is the culprit, it exonerates all homesellers (since they are no longer being subtly assaulted as being "solely responsible" for their fate) due to the fact that they are not responsible for the marketing. This also leads to a careful assessment of all "P's" (which contextualizes the "Pricing P"), making changes more acceptable and again, contextual. This gives you more to review with them.

Real Estate Professional: "Do you still have an open mind regarding different marketing ideas? Great!"

Explanation:

• This is a premise not relevant to any professional whose career-mantra is "homes either sell or don't sell solely based upon price."

• This more sensitive and strategic communication emerges out of a feeling of empowerment and from the knowledge that you provide greater value (and possesses immense inner self-respect) based upon your mastery of "The Four P's of Marketing" ... all on behalf of and for the benefit of your clients.

Real Estate Professional: "I've been waiting to call you for weeks but couldn't contact you until today due to our Code of Ethics."

Explanation:
• This repositions you from one being overly aggressive to one who now appears to be exercising restraint and playing by the rules.

Homeowner: "Why didn't YOU sell my home while it was listed?"

Real Estate Professional: "Because I didn't have the right buyer for your property, which is not surprising because it would be statistically unlikely that I, out of 3,000 other Realtors®, would have been the right person with the right buyer... but really the more important question is 'Why didn't someone out of 3,000 Realtors® *bring* the *right* buyer?' And to me there's only one answer to that... and that's how your property was marketed. If you still have an open mind about other marketing ideas, I'd like to come by and show you how we can upgrade your marketing."

Please remember that since Price is part of Marketing, it enables you to (very forcibly) say two things to Expired listing homesellers:

• "There's only one reason your home didn't sell... Marketing!"
• "I'd like to come by and show you how we can upgrade your marketing."
Contrasted to these alternatives:

• "There's only one reason your home didn't sell. It was overpriced."
• "I'd like to come by and show you how we can reduce your price. When's a good time?"

This also means that you must disengage from the century-old (and absurd) Industry teaching that:

"The Buyer Determines the Price."

No, the buyer, buying-side Realtor®, the homeseller, the homeseller Realtor®, the appraiser, and the lender all have a role in determining a final and fully negotiated price.

I think some of you recently learned in the short sale market that Lenders also play a role in determining the price.

70

Question: How could we possibly not understand that homesellers are exactly like lenders who own properties and they too have a say (to say the least) in determining the price? Thank God this is so! For if we were a "commodity" where only one side, the buyer or the market, determined the price then we too would be paid a seven dollar commission for a million dollar sale... just like E*Trade.

Something tells me that this is not how you want to connect your value within your community.

I strongly suggest that you become appreciative that the buyer alone does not determine price. Why? Because if either side of a Real Estate transaction is solely responsible for the pricing outcome, then compensation could never be logically attributed to at least one of the two sides. That would be absurd! Not to mention homeowners having to accept why thousands, or tens of thousands of dollars, are being paid to a professional who plays no role in the financial outcome!

By merely accepting this "intellectually lazy conclusion" (that the buyer alone determines the price) in my view makes you less prepared to confidently and more respectfully engage "Expired-listing homesellers." In other words: "Why don't we just lower the price and keep our same Realtor®" equals a lack of respect for what you truly do and deserve more credit for.

This is because a "Listing Agent" (versus a "Marketing Realtor®") who believes that homes don't sell principally because of price and, even then, holds that the buyer determines that price, is essentially diminishing the enormous value of their Negotiating, Networking, Marketing, and Merchandising/Staging.
And, when you put your vast skill-set behind more respectful and optimistic communication (becoming a prodigious prospector within the "Expired listing" homeseller community) the following occurs: A deeply committed devotion to Marketing excellence – making it a joy and celebration for you when you present your value to homesellers.

The Community of Homesellers pays a heavy premium (in the form of fees) for you to impact their outcomes. The more you believe that you truly upgrade marketing (including how you also market the town, city, or neighborhood they live in), and the more you respect what you do the more you, in turn, will respect both For Sale By Owner and Expired listing members of the community.

Since *Creating Real Estate Connections* is a book (and not our online certification course), we are limited in how much detail and interaction we can provide in this publication.

Throughout our *Certified Community Marketing Specialist*SM course (leading to a privileged and well-deserved designation), we will present much greater practical details, scripts regarding BOTH of these niche markets, and all other segmented Real Estate-relevant, community-based engagement precepts and systems.

For Now, Here are a Few "Insider Tips"

For years when calling on For Sale By Owners (which I did most Sunday or Monday evenings for twenty years for my own company... and then gave my associates leads), I used to express the following:

For Sale By Oner Cold-Call Suggested Script

Real Estate Professional: "Hi, I'm calling from our company's For Sale By Owner Division."

Explanation:
• Homesellers saw this as an affirmation that their status was important enough for us to have a division!

Homeowner: "You are the twentieth person to call!"

Real Estate Professional: "I'm sorry to hear that. Let me come over so we can put an end to that."

Homeowner: "Can you just mail me the information?"

Real Estate Professional: "The most important information is me... and I don't fit in the mail. Let's get together. I love the outside of your home and the great street you live on. So, let's give more people a chance to fight over your home!"

Chapter Summary

We must all appreciate that language is the "clothing of ideas." This means that the words we select express our thoughts and feelings and when we are not careful with them we can alienate consumers and prospective clients.

There is arguably no situation where consumers are more sensitive to precisely what is being said then when they are in the process of being "Expired listing homeowners" and "For Sale By Owners." Please remember that, in both these circumstances, it is not just a matter of displaying respect but also of how effective you are at demonstrating value. For example: When prematurely attempting to convince an Expired listing homeowner of how great you are in Real Estate, at a time when they blame the entire Real Estate community for its collective failure to sell their home, it might come across as "I'm the best at what you hate... I'm King Rat!"

Accordingly, I suggest you carefully consider the scripting I provided you with in this chapter and, if you employ it, you will find this kinder, gentler, and more sophisticated, professional approach to solving their problem is significantly better received.

Chapter 6

<u>Working Only with Homesellers</u>
<u>Through Local Media and Marketing</u>
an interview with Russell Shaw
Ranked #28 Top Producing Realtor® Nationally by Realtor® Magazine
by Gee Dunsten

Russell Shaw:

Russell of Realty ONE/Russell Shaw Group has been in the Real Estate business since 1978, starting with John Hall & Associates and transferring over to Realty ONE Group in 2011. He has ranked among the top 1% of all agents in the United States since 1991. He has been recognized by the National Association of Realtors® as being among the top 50 agents nationally for number of homes sold and by the Wall Street Journal as being among the Top 200 Agents in America.

He has been a featured speaker many times at the national convention for Certified Residential Specialists and has also spoken at the National Association of Realtors® convention, as well as routinely speaking at various state association conventions.

Russell was a part of the first study of its kind, ever – real research being done at the university level on lead generation.

He is featured in the book, "Billion Dollar Agent" and was featured and quoted extensively in the best selling book, by Gary Keller, "The Millionaire Real Estate Agent." Even though not with that company, Russell has repeatedly contributed to the curriculum for Keller Williams University.

Favorite Quote:

"Vision is the art of seeing things invisible" – Jonathan Swift

Gee Dunsten:

When did you get into the Real Estate business?

Russell Shaw:

I started in 1978, so I have been marketing and selling homes for 36 years.

G. Dunsten:

Why did you get into this crazy business?

R. Shaw:

Actually, I didn't know what else to do. When I surveyed my options it seemed to be the best choice. In the first twelve years, I really struggled, living deal to deal, closing to closing. Most of my work was with buyers, doing 17 to 22 transactions per year. According to industry standards at the time, that was supposed to be good, but I was always living paycheck to paycheck. I didn't have any idea what I was doing and once in a while a listing got dumped in my lap. I didn't know how to price the property or how to list it, although I thought I knew what I was doing. In 1985, I decided to get some training. Between 1985 and 1986, I got my GRI and my CRS. The most important thing I learned was that the top agents –the excellent ones – were geographic farmers and great listers.

G. Dunsten:
So what did you do?

R. Shaw:
At that point, I thought if I was going to stay in this business and really become successful, I would have to get all the way in or all the way out and find a different career path. I decided to burn all my bridges in working with buyers. My first step was to cancel all of our buyer ads. I told Wendy that we were stopping our work with buyers and were going to focus 100% of our efforts on getting listings instead. We could not afford to be distracted by buyers, and I never wanted to take another buyer out again and since 1993, I haven't.

G. Dunsten:
What happened?

R. Shaw:
From that point on, we only went after listings. We tried every stupid thing we could think of. I tried different kinds of scripts, different types of approaches, and we showed up, which was the only thing we did do right! All of our listings were overpriced.

G. Dunsten:
Did focusing 100% on listings increase your transactions?

R. Shaw:
Yes, Gee, they did. We went from 17 transactions per year to 38 closings per year and as we began to get better, our success rate improved.

G. Dunsten:
What was the tipping point to increasing your volume?

R. Shaw:
Our biggest breakthrough occurred when we started doing radio and our production increased to 60+ transactions. Part of my background was doing commercials for others, so I approached the radio station and agreed to help with the writing and producing of comedy in exchange for 10 free ads per week.

G. Dunsten:
How did it work out?

76

R. Shaw:

Well, it actually took me a year to get the phone to ring. At first, I thought the station was not actually running my ad. In fact, one day while I was at the station, I went into the booth and confronted the "jock" and asked him why he was not running my ads? He quickly informed me that he had just run one of our ads in the last 15 minutes. When we got our first ad call, I wanted to know what things in the ad were good and what made her call us. She told me that it was the opportunity to cancel the listing if they weren't satisfied.

G. Dunsten:

How long ago was that?

R. Shaw:

I think it was late 1989 or early 1990. In fact, within the next 30 days, based on what we heard, the basis for our ads evolved into what we are basically still doing today.

G. Dunsten:

So you reinvented your ads. Did you stay with the same free radio station?

R. Shaw:

No, we didn't. At that time, the station was sold to someone else and in structuring what they were doing, we lost the free ad deal. Wendy, asked what we were going to do and I told her we would have to buy some ads. It was the very best thing that could have happened. By losing the deal, and changing stations, our business jumped to 60 deals. So, we tried two different stations on a trial basis and we ran our new ads using my voice instead of someone else's at the radio station. We spent $1000 per month with each one and clearly, the "talk radio" station was the best. That year we spent just over $20,000 with them, which resulted in a little over 100 deals.

G. Dunsten:

With that major jump in business, what did you do next?

R. Shaw:

Actually, the next year we signed a $40,000 contract that resulted in 130 deals. I thought that was fantastic! It was like printing money. So, the next year we signed an $80,000 contract.

G. Dunsten:

Wow! What was the result?

R. Shaw:

Gee, that was the year we learned about the "Law of Diminishing Returns." We got the same results, but lost $40,000. Although expensive, it was a great lesson. It forced me to become a better student of my business and I learned how to become a media buyer. As a result, we hired a second station and later we added a third.

G. Dunsten:

What type of radio station works the best?

R. Shaw:

That's a great question. We've tried them all. First, let's talk about what doesn't work. Country Western, soft jazz, and sports stations don't work. I can't tell you why. All I know is they don't lead to listings.

G. Dunsten:

Which ones do work best and why?

R. Shaw:

Talk Radio is absolutely the best, because data is the entertainment for the listening audience. Depending upon your target audience, Classic Rock and Oldies can also work. I know this through trial and error and having spent thousands of dollars. In 2006, we took over 600 listings.

G. Dunsten:

What are the biggest problems agents face today?

R. Shaw:

Almost every agent experiences the same two problems:
1. Getting to the table with the homeowner
2. Getting the listing under the correct terms and conditions

G. Dunsten:

As the #1 agent in Phoenix, and with all your success and experience, I bet you get almost every listing you go after, right?

R. Shaw:

I'm glad you asked me that question, Gee. Actually, the answer is no. In fact, we get less than half. In other words, for every 100 appointments we go on, we take/ accept 45 listings.

G. Dunsten:
Really? Why is that?

R. Shaw:
Because it's not about getting the listing, it's about selling their home. It's about expectations, cooperation, motivation, and creating a partnership with the same goal. Actually, with only a few exceptions, every top listing agent turns down more seller listing opportunities than they take.

G. Dunsten:
Russell, that is great information for our readers. With all your success, tell me about your experience with television.

R. Shaw:
Sure, Gee. After a number of years, we kind of maxed out our market penetration with radio. Obviously, the best media to use to build trust and establish rapport is TV, however when we first started out in TV, it was a huge failure. To be honest, it's taken a great deal of effort to finally reach a place where it's working for us.

G. Dunsten:
So, what have you learned?

R. Shaw:
A number of things. First, the best place to be seen is on a national and/or local News segment. The News is live and sticky and the viewers are looking for data and information. They might be interested in CSI and will quickly go to the fridge during a commercial or they TIVO the show to watch later so they can fast forward through the commercials. People don't TIVO the News because they watch to see it LIVE!

Your delivery, as well as, the quality of your information is more than half the battle for recognition and credibility on TV. It's extremely important to make sure that you're transmitting a friendly, approachable, energetic, believable message to your viewers in a few seconds. Things like proper lighting, your wardrobe, background, colors, and most importantly, your facial expression, are huge. Make sure you have a friend, team member, or family member acting as your executive producer when your ad is being recorded, instead of a camera guy who is more concerned with capturing and framing what is seen on the screen, rather than the effectiveness of your delivery. Ask your friend to be a critical observer. Are you smiling, energetic, believable? How is your tonality and posture? It can be very powerful when the verbal message and the visual message go together. TV is more powerful, but it takes more effort to make it work. It's harder to get your part right for your target audience.

G. Dunsten:

What about local critics?

R. Shaw:

It doesn't really matter what other agents, family members, or some of your friends say. It isn't important, especially if they aren't a representative of your target audience.

G. Dunsten:

How long should you run an ad to determine whether it's working?

R. Shaw:

With radio, you should know in 1-2 weeks. If you are not causing a reaction from the people (listeners), you have a problem with the station, ad copy, or delivery. The larger the audience you are reaching, the faster you will know.

G. Dunsten:

What other things have you learned?

R. Shaw:

10 p.m. News works, but it is a lot more money. Depending on your target audience, for a lot less money and a lot more exposure, the 5 a.m. News might prove to be more profitable.

You have to think people. For example, we don't want to attract the millennials or those between 18 and 35 years of age, because they don't have houses to sell. We want to attract 65-year-olds, so we select stations that appeal most to people with gray hair! We're not trying to reach homebuyers. In fact, buyers won't respond to radio. Houses appeal to buyers. They don't want to look for an agent. Sellers are the only ones that want to find an agent. The seller pays for the agent and they shop for their agent. In fact, most sellers don't talk to more than one agent.

All agent problems are related to two things; how to get to the table to interview the seller and how effective you are once you get to the table.

G. Dunsten:

What are the major differences in working with buyers versus sellers?

R. Shaw:

Most agents don't realize the difference in working with buyers and working with sellers. Working with buyers is relationship-based. It's about building trust, rapport, and making

80

the home search and home tours not only positive, but fun. All our communications are about them. It's about harvesting information and at the same time, maintaining likability. Working with sellers is presentation-based. Are you competent? Can you get the job done? Working the buyer side is more fun, more sociable, like a party. Working the listing side is hard work, more tedious, lonely. It involves working more evenings and coming home late. It's more detailed and requires a task-based approach. It takes the ability to know and work numbers and analyze data.

G. Dunsten:
What lessons have you learned?

R. Shaw:
Many agents think they can get lots of listing business from Zillow, Facebook, Trulia, etc., when in reality we really don't. To have a successful business, you must be listing-based. Most of your business must be coming from the listing side. You need to be a geographical farmer type of person. In reality, the only way to generate business is through marketing and prospecting. Both are very important.

Successful agents:
1. Get the listing
2. Sell the listing
3. Often get buyers without trying

Listings generate buyers. Buyers don't generate listings.

G. Dunsten:
Russell, you've shared a lot of information and a lot of great ideas. In closing, please share your words of wisdom.

R. Shaw:
Learn to listen. Set your ego aside and admit that you don't know everything. The biggest barrier is the false idea that we know how to effectively talk to sellers. Most agents do only 8-10 presentations per year. You must get on the stage, so you can do more and more presentations.

Practice with your family, friends, and co-workers. When possible, get in front of sellers where you don't really care if you get the listing or not. You might need to make appointments 25 miles away so you can practice on 6-10 listing prospects. Find out the kinds of things sellers want to know and the kinds of things they think they know but aren't necessarily correct. Figure out what to say and how to better express yourself.

81

The purpose of the listing appointment is not to take the listing, but rather to decide if you want to take the listing. You only want to select those you want to sell. You want to know that not only will you be successful, but that you will enjoy the opportunity of working together with the seller.

The key is to get better at lead generation, so you can go on appointments without being worried about the outcome and turn down listings without any remorse. Most of us start out not knowing anything. Actually, we're pretty crappy. The more we do, the less crappy we get, until one day, we get good!

Dalton's Take-away:

When I first met Russell he, on behalf of all Realtors® in America, actually "took me on" in a very personal fashion, regarding our Realtor.com pricing model. I learned very quickly that Russell is willing to fight for what he believes in, his fellow Realtors® and the community he represents. Russell is a winner in every sense of the word.

Chapter 7

Advocating for Your State
an interview with Rei Mesa
Berkshire Hathaway HomeServices Florida Realty CEO

by Allan Dalton

Rei Mesa:

Rei Mesa is President and CEO of Berkshire Hathaway HomeServices Florida Realty.

Both a Certified Residential Specialist (CRS) and Certified Residential Broker (CRB) Rei Also serves as a National Association of Realtors® (NAR) Director and serves on the NAR® Executive Committee.

Mesa, a District 4 Trustee for RPAC, has also served as Director of the National Association of Hispanic Real Estate Professionals.

Favorite Quote(s):

"The best index to a person's character is how he treats people who cannot do him any good and how he treats people who cannot fight back." – Abigail Van Buren

---

Allan Dalton:

Rei, to most in Real Estate, the concept of 'community' means either a local town, city or neighborhood... or is representative of a specialized group such as 'African American' or 'Irish American', etc. To you, however, the meaning of "community" also seems to extend to the entire state; which, in your case, is Florida.

Rei Mesa:

My deep and eternal love and passion for Florida, perhaps more than any other reason, is due to my parents.

Since they emigrated from Cuba to America, it is understandable that, when they dreamt and then planned to move to America, Florida (approximately a hundred miles away) was 'the gateway'.

Therefore, Florida has always been viewed by them (and by me) as a life-transformative and sacred location representing freedom, opportunities, blessed diversity, amazing communities, world-renowned beaches, and perpetual Sunshine.

A. Dalton:

How has your reverence for 'The Sunshine State' influenced how you have built and led your Real Estate organization?

R. Mesa:

That is an important question, Allan. For starters, it has meant that my company, unlike almost all other Real Estate Companies across the Country, has embedded in our Company Brand Name... the inclusion of the state name.

This is why, when we transformed our Company Brand and Real Estate culture recently (by becoming a proud member of the Berkshire Hathaway HomeServices esteemed network) we ensured that we would continue with our state-specific company name as part of our overall brand.

A. Dalton:

Rei, knowing you, every decision you make for your company must comport with your relentless dedication to serving your entire state. How did this influence your selecting Berkshire Hathaway HomeServices to partner with?

R. Mesa:

It did so in multiple ways. First, since our existing culture celebrated how we market Florida Real Estate at the highest level, it was important that we had a brand that was consistent with that 'mantra'... and Berkshire Hathaway HomeServices pedigree suggests elevated respect, service, and skill.

Secondly, we needed a brand with a level of sophistication necessary in relating to our wide and eclectic range of buyers and investors.

Since Florida is a worldwide, coveted destination (over and above our steady stream of buyers and investors from the Northeast, Midwest and Canada), it compelled us to be associated with a brand that conveys both national and international 'gravitas'.

And lastly, one must never forget that, given the jokes of yesteryear about 'being sold swampland in Florida', trust (although important everywhere) is especially important here in Florida... and no brand is more emblematic of trust and financial rectitude, in my view, than Berkshire Hathaway HomeServices.

And, given how Florida was significantly impacted by the Real Estate down-turn of the recent past, bringing the Berkshire Hathaway HomeServices brand to Florida sends a powerful and most stabilizing subliminal message.

A. Dalton:

Rei, I'm glad that you used the word subliminal because, I must confess, that in all my years, I have never heard a consumer exclaim that they are looking for a Real Estate company that stands for 'financial rectitude'... but I get your point.

But seriously, Rei, I've never seen any other Real Estate Company whose identity and culture is as state-specific as yours is.

Now, I am sure some of this is understandable as some of the greatest companies in North America serve multiple states (such as Weichert, Long and Foster, John L. Scott, etc.) preventing them from going all-in for any one state... and, most other companies only cover 'regions' or 'metropolitan areas'.

I love how you have so visibly leveraged your very special, geographical relationship to your state. How deliberate a strategy has this been?

R. Mesa:
Very. We have a two-fold, state-specific strategy for our Company.

I constantly encourage all of our Company Associates and Local Managers to principally focus on their local communities... as each of our local Florida communities are distinct and represent varying demographics and local cultures.

Consequently, it is not the job of my Managers or Realtor® Associates to primarily 'Market the State'.

That's my job as the Company leader. Specifically, to present our company to our Associates, Management, the Media and to North America's Real Estate Community, as representing Florida holistically and as an incomparable lifestyle destination. Again, that is my job.

A. Dalton:
Rei, how do you do that?

R. Mesa:
One way is by combining my love for Florida, its Real Estate, and my enduring passion for the National Association of Realtors®.

This is my way of prospecting for referrals and businesses for our company and our state... and it has worked enormously well.

This means that every time I speak at National Conventions, every panel I am invited to participate in, every focus group on how the National Association of Realtors® can best serve the Industry's larger Brokerages, I constantly speak to the Real Estate opportunities in Florida.

How can I expect my Associates to prospect for local business, if I (as their leader) am not similarly prospecting? But, in this case, 'painting on a larger canvas'... such as relocation firms, etc.

Most companies in Florida (or Brokers) cannot assume this role, as they do not enjoy broad enough geographical coverage... in order to speak on behalf of the whole state as one single Brokerage entity.

A. Dalton:
What do you mean by that, Rei?

R. Mesa:
Brokers from the northeast don't want to hear another broker asking for all of their referrals to Florida when they only serve one region.

We offer vast coverage and complete 'one-stop shopping'. Brokers and Realtors®... and especially consumers... value this.

A. Dalton:
Rei, speak to how you're being a former National Director for the Hispanic Association of Realtors® also helps you enhance your broad-based Florida appeal.

R. Mesa:
Allan, Florida is wonderously diverse... and I want to be able to relate to all of our different and very nuanced markets.

This is one of the reasons why my wife and I have residences on both Florida coasts... as it allows me to keep 'my hand on the pulse' of these two distinctive lifestyles.

Regarding the Hispanic Real Estate Community:

We are blessed at our company to have attracted a significant percentage of high-quality Associates who are also Hispanic. The value of this, especially when serving those who speak Spanish and our heavy percentage of South American investors, is immense.

A. Dalton:
What is the Number One Florida community-wide charity you support?

87

R. Mesa:

Allan, that would be our company-wide dedication, and ongoing devotion, to The Sunshine Kids Foundation.

Although this tremendously important cause (one that reaches out to young children with acute and heart-wrenching needs) goes well beyond Florida, I must confess that we support numerous charities and encourage our Associates to support as many as they are able to... that the name 'Sunshine Kids' made this charity even more appealing – because we want everyone to have as sunny a life as possible... and especially our children. This year my offices raised $300,000 (and Berkshire Hathaway Home Services nationwide $2.5 Million) for this worthy cause. I believe this is consistent with how generous our Industry is compared to all of the industries which directly impact local communities.

I want every individual and family member in the entire state of Florida, when they think of Florida Real Estate, to think of Berkshire HomesServices Florida Realty.

A. Dalton:

What else do you do to ensure that Florida is your company's primary community?

R. Mesa:

When I hire managers, I look for how deep their passion and loyalty is regarding our state and explain to them how Florida competes with other states for business... and we need to keep 'winning'.

A. Dalton:

How long have you been beating this Florida drum?

R. Mesa:

For as long as I have been in business... but it intensified several years ago for two reasons:

First, our home values dropped dramatically, causing some buyers who typically move to Florida to choose other states... which meant that we needed to put 'Florida living' in an even more positive perspective than ever.

The other reason had to do with an interview I watched on Meet the Press years ago which featured Mayor Bloomberg.

The New York Mayor was asked, "What is the biggest threat to the economic future of New York City?" His answer floored me. He responded with, "That would be London."

His explanation was, "We are fighting for the same people to move and work here."

I had two reactions. One was to call him and tell him he should move to Florida (as we do not compete with London) and my other thought was that I want to do for my state what civic leaders, Governors and mayors try to do for their cities and states... become a passionate and effective advocate for Florida.

A. Dalton:
Rei, I know you to be one of the most passionate and loyal brokers in America, and, while you have been named as one of the top executives in the Industry by multiple publications, I have never once observed you calling attention to yourself. Instead, it's Florida, Berkshire Hathaway HomeServices, your Alma Mater University of Miami Hurricanes, the Dolphins, the Miami Heat, and the many regions where you serve... yet no community commands any more respect from you than the National Association of Realtors®. Why such a deep bond?

R. Mesa:
My entire business career is based upon one unmistakable reality: I cannot accomplish anything alone. My success can only be through teamwork.

Not just my teamwork, with my our parent company, our executive and Senior Management teams and our entire family of Realtor® Associates, but also, I know in my heart that I could never have enjoyed whatever success I might be able to point to... were it not for being a Realtor®.

Becoming a Realtor® was the single most important business decision of my entire career.

What I have learned through CRS and CRB courses, large Broker meetings, along with all I have learned from our state and national conventions, has deeply guided my business life.

Recently, I was asked by Dale Stinton and Bob Goldberg (the top executives with NAR®) to speak to the NAR® VIP group of Alliance Partners that Bob Goldberg has strategically and sensitively put together to benefit every Realtor®.

I was so proud when these 'outside of our Industry Executives' in person told me how much they respect how hard we Realtors® work and the important role we play in the lives of consumers.

89

This type of respect would never exist without all of us working side by side and collaborating on behalf of fellow consumer clients. Such collaboration could never take place without the organizational genius of the National Association of Realtors®.

A. Dalton:
Any last word?

R. Mesa:
Let me say this, I want to continue building our company on this premise: 'One must be able to believe in things bigger than oneself'. For me, that's our state, our Brand, our Association, and all those we serve... and for us, that means the 'Community of Florida'.

And, if I may (and most respectfully) offer any advice to my fellow Brokers through-out the Industry, our leadership responsibilities must not only include the evangelical treatment of our great Real Estate Brands (whether it be BHHS, Better Homes and Gardens, Century 21, Coldwell Banker, ERA, Exit Realty, Keller Williams, ReMax, Sotheby's International Realty, etc. Allan, I've listed them alphabetically and realize there are many others) but, in addition to the passion we place behind these brands, we must also be the leaders regarding the respect displayed for our local communities – be they neighborhoods, towns, cities and our states... and Florida Communities one and all.

A. Dalton:
Rei, what do you suggest that smaller Brokers do that don't have offices throughout their entire state to create more connectivity within their state?

R. Mesa:
Even a one office company or, for that matter, a single Realtor in a one office company, can always advertise the following: "We'll market the best state in America to call home..." That's how everybody should think and it is a common denominator that every home-owner in their state, even if it is only that one town, will be impressed with.

A. Dalton:
Thank you, Rei, for believing in the importance of *Creating Real Estate Connections*... .a goal which you epitomize.

Dalton's Take-away:

Rei Mesa, during a period of time where his state's home values were being ravaged and his company was going through a complete brand change (by selecting Berkshire Hathaway HomeServices), managed to steer his company ship through these challenging times... and is now moving forward with power-boat speed; a movement that begins and ends with his indomitable spirit, leadership, infectious enthusiasm, and love for the state of Florida.

Chapter 8

How Community-centric Systems Grew my Company from 5 to over 50 Offices
by Allan Dalton

Co-founder, TownAdvisor.com & Former CEO of Realtor.com

Truth be told, I have never been interested in offering any advice on any subject to fellow professionals that I have not personally tested. Therefore, let me offer what I have done in my Real Estate brokerage career that may be of value to you.

I must say that without these experiences I would never presume to bring this book to the Industry; never mind have my picture and name along with Gee Dunsten's on the front cover. Indeed, there is no substitute for experiential knowledge and no greater responsibility than in what you suggest others to do; especially suggestions which can influence career and livelihood decisions, strategies, and outcomes. This is why I have immense respect for Gee Dunsten. Gee has amazingly combined serving as past president of CRS while remaining, to this day, one of America's most successful practicing community-based Realtors®.

While I deeply respect Gee, I must acknowledge that I revere industry-icons Jim Weichert and Dick Schlott. I laud Jim Weichert and Dick Schlott because, if not for their immense greatness, I would never have discovered the importance of attempting to reach the community as I did and in ways that dramatically differentiated our much smaller company.

You see, when I moved from Boston to New Jersey to become a partner of my mentor and personal hero, Joe Murphy at Murphy Realty Better Homes and Gardens, our company of fifteen years (yet only possessing five offices) was competing in Northern New Jersey with two of the three largest independent brokerages in the history of the entire world (that's right the entire world) along with Wes Foster and his iconic Long and Foster.

In contrast to our five office company, both Weichert and Schlott each had grown to over one hundred offices in the State of New Jersey alone (the very state where they launched their soon-to-be mega-companies). How could we compete within the seventy-one towns (just in our one county) for listings; never mind grow against these "monolithic octopuses?"

With my partner and mentor's, Joe Murphy's, complete support, both financially and emotionally (Joe always had my back), I created these four following community-based programs and systems which became the basis of our culture and fueled our subsequent growth. These community-based systems represented an overarching strategy, one responsible for taking us to twenty consecutive years of considerable profit and growth and to more than fifty offices.

Community-based Idea #1: You Don't Have to Beat Them if You Join Them... When They Don't Join You!

I began to take out full page ads in all of the community newspapers that informed the entire community that, when they selected our company, they were selecting the entire Real Estate community.

I called my system "The Better Homes and Gardens Home Marketing System," which became a franchise which I later sold the rights to for national usage along with four additional systems which I sold to Better Homes and Gardens Real Estate Service in the following years.

The four systems were:

The Better Homes and Gardens:
- ...Home Information System
- ...Home Marketing System
- ...Marketing Upgrade System, and
- ...Home Buying System

"I eliminated all competition... by including them!"

Allan Dalton presented the Home Merchandising System at Convention

All four National Marketing Systems were highly successful, but it was the Home Marketing System which immediately registered within all of our communities and here's why:

Our major competitors were not even bringing up our company's name when they met with homesellers by explaining that our company was part of their company's marketing team.

Conversely, our entire theme was that all of the other competitors were part of our marketing team (as reflected in our full page local ads). At that time, unbelievably, these other companies were only saying that they belonged to the MLS – which meant that they cooperated with the other companies (as if it were a minor afterthought). I made sure that this celebration of collaboration was our monumental message.

What homeowner doesn't want to believe that the entire Real Estate Industry is marketing their property? What possibly could be a bigger message than that? It's like, why wouldn't anyone want to leverage the greatness of what the NAR® has made possible for all Realtors®? It was simple, a Real Estate community message for the consumer community.

Today, many brokerages make the same present-day mistake when it comes to their explanation of the Internet. They are actually more willing to show a visual illustration of how Zillow, Trulia, Realtor.com, and The Wall Street Journal (etc.) are all part of their Internet team, but they don't include ColdwellBanker.com, ReMax.com, SothebysRealty.com, KellerWilliams.com, Weichert.com, and ExitRealty.com (etc.); even though these collaborative Real Estate brokerages have much more to do with any one company's marketing process, and therefore, have much more to do with either gaining or losing the listing.

**"How do you eliminate competitor websites...
by including them!"**

The name of the game is:

"The best way to eliminate the competition is by including them!"

Again, what I did was take a Real Estate community approach to the community... and then customized it. Strangely, most companies still can't point to a specifically branded system for their marketing. I was able to (later on) sell my idea to Century 21, where we created the Century 21 Customized Home Marketing System, to ERA, where we created the Value Added Marketing System, and to NRT (Coldwell Banker), where we introduced (nationally) the Coldwell Banker Full Service Marketing System.

I'll never forget the first time I introduced all the other companies in an ad with our sign and Joe Murphy in the middle. It was at a meeting where I invited Mike Ferry to come speak. After the meeting Mike said, "Allan, I'm coming out with a book *How to Make a Six Figure Income in Real Estate* and your idea to advertise full-page ads in local newspapers with your competition blows my mind so much, I'd like to dedicate the book to you." Which he did.

Interestingly, I so-called "subsumed my competition" long before Coke had Pepsi in their ads and Burger King had MacDonald's. My thinking was (and still is), "Why not walk the prospect through all of their options while you are with them and in control?"

The key, however, is to make sure your Associates present this in a matter-of-fact fashion and not suspiciously competitive. Also I should point out that merely by having a brand name for our system (The Home Marketing System), we did what MacDonald's did. That is, instead of selling two all-beef patties, special sauce, etc., they sell a "Big Mac" and instead of selling an Open House, MLS, advertising, CMA, Feature Sheets, etc., we were now selling a "Real Estate Big Mac" –something that the Real Estate community could relate to and trust.

You need to brand all of your services and systems in a distinctive way.

For example, what would you say (or all of your Associates) if asked the following questions by a community member:

• "What is the name of your system or program for buyers?"
• "What is the specifically branded name for how your company markets properties?"

Moreover, while essentially every Real Estate company in North America (these days) provides their Associates with an "Internet wheel" (which includes Realtor.com, Zillow, and Trulia), they miss the much bigger point.

Let me put it this way... When was the last time one of your Associates lost a listing to Zillow, Trulia, Realtor.com or the Wall Street Journal? Try never. Instead, they lose listings to other companies. The answer to this problem: Provide your Associates with an illustration that includes your competitors *(see previous exhibits).*

I still have a strong sense that exceptional companies like Remax, Keller Williams, or Sotheby's International Realty Associates (by way of example) do not enthusiastically say and show homeowners how ColdwellBanker.com is an important part of their Online Marketing System. Rather, all they do is instead mention IDX.

Without showing a circle with "their dot com" in the middle, and all other local and national Realtor® websites serving as satellites, the verbalization of IDX is lost. How many Realtors® completely grasped the meaning of IDX in the first two minutes it was explained to them?

How does that expression go? *One picture is worth what...?* If ever there was a need for a picture of the Real Estate community for the community, this is it.

Remember:
• The more you try to convince them that you are different, the more they are compelled to research the difference.
• The more you include your community competition, the more you eliminate them as possibilities.

Little wonder why some homesellers still feel a need to see what other firms do online because this industry-community approach becomes secondary to self-serving render- ings of one's own company site (even though more exposure comes from the collective). Truly remarkable!

By explaining to homesellers that, "The web is all about Range, Reach, and Influence. Range and Reach are completely taken care of by me and my competitors/collabora- tors," you eliminate all competition and now are only left with influence. *(See Town Advisor: "Everyone else just markets homes. Here's how we specifically market your town too!")*

Community-based Idea #2: Multicultural Marketing

Years ago Joe Murphy and I created Buyers Guides in five different languages: Chinese, Korean, Russian, Spanish, and English.

Not only was this our greatest differentiator (as other companies didn't do four-color Homes Guides in Russian, Spanish, etc. Weichert, for example, had one hundred offices... which is why they were a great part of our system), but Homesellers could not take their hands or eyes off these multicultural magazines.

Now this was twenty years ago. So is this idea now outdated? I guess if your company is already doing Buyers Guides in Russian, Spanish, Korean, and Chinese, yes. If not, consider doing it immediately.

"We published four color Homes Guides in five different languages. Here's two examples."

We would explain to homesellers that, "Most of these buyers did not need these guides, as they could speak English, but it showed respect and symbolically extended a 'Multicultural Welcome Mat' in front of your homes to a bigger buyer pool." In our multicultural market this community-ecumenical idea resonated resoundingly well. Capiche?

The greatest use of our distinct Community Guides however, was among developers.

Joe and I personally listed "Newport at Jersey City" (with the famed LeFrac family), a potential ten thousand unit condo listing... and dominated the representation of "Gold Coast developments overlooking Manhattan." It was either Joe and I or Charlie Oppler (now co-owner of Prominent Properties Sotheby's International Realty and past president of the New Jersey Association of Realtors®) who secured all of these mega complexes.

98

Joe and I succeeded uniquely, however... as the builders and developers were blown away by our multicultural marketing and community connections.

Community-based Idea #3: State Slogan

The classic definition of marketing (for me) is: "You first determine the unmet needs of the market (community) and then you create goods and services to satisfy those needs."

This enthusiastically adopted principle (by me) subsequently lead to the next community-based idea that I am happy to share. Years ago when writing a paper in a collegiate marketing course I wrote, "The only way we have access to people is through their concerns." My professor underlined my words and wrote, "Excellent point!"
With such an affirmation, I have repeated that statement for decades. And, since no one has told me it doesn't make sense, I will again use it as a preface to my following community connectivity-based point: "The only way we have access to people is through their concerns, and New Jersey homeowners are all concerned about the perception of their state and its home values."

If we were going to do materially more to "marketize our larger community," it must begin with this question: What does every homeowner in the state of New Jersey have in common? The answer is incontrovertible. They all want to see their home values grow.

Second question: What is the one thing above all others that collectively relates to all state home values beyond property condition and location? Again, incontrovertible answer: The perception of the state.

And seeing how New Jersey homeowners do not think all of the New Jersey jokes are as funny as their compatriots in the forty-nine other states, why not do something that promotes the entire state and thus all homeowners' interests? In other words, why not attempt to connect with the community in the two deepest ways possible:

• Their home values
• The desire to have the state they call home be better respected

In other words instead of saying, "We are number one," I decided to leave that crowded campaign to our competitors and instead started advertising that New Jersey is the number one state to live in in America *(see TownAdvisor.com)*. Better yet, I created a slogan. The slogan juxtapositioned neighboring (and intensely competitive)

New York; home to many of the slights directed at our beloved Garden State.

I actually subsumed the old, unofficial New York slogan, "New York is a great place to visit, but I wouldn't want to live there," with "New Jersey is a great place to visit, and an even greater place to live!"

The slogan became viral. Thousands of state residents asked for the bumper sticker, which included our company logo, and New Jersey Senator Frank Lautenberg asked if he could have a picture taken with Joe and me for the newspapers.

"Joe Murphy and I were thrilled that a US Senator (Senator Lautenberg, NJ) wanted to help promote our company slogan."

My message to you is: "Your state is a community ready to be Marketized!"

When was the last time residents asked *you* for a bumper sticker of yours that they could put on the back of their automobile reading: "Spouses selling Houses," or "List with Us and start Packing," or "We're the Home Team?"

Next, I personally had to sign releases with several tourism bureaus, as they used my slogan in their county brochures. But unfortunately, my efforts did very little to diminish the (later on) depictions of New Jersey made famous by *The Sopranos* and Snookie, but it did help.

Our company grew from five to over fifty offices (thirty-two that Joe and I owned, and twenty plus that we franchised), all in a two year period before we sold the company.

Community-based Idea #4: Real Estate Town Meetings^{SM}

A final, for now, community-based idea that we built our company on was Real Estate Town Meetings^{SM}

100

I was never enthralled by the conventional approach of Real Estate companies to engage the community via public events or seminars. You know, the typical buyer's seminar where one brings in a mortgage rep., lawyer, home inspector, stager, etc., while using the nomenclature of "buyer's night." Thus, I created what I called Real Estate Town Meetings^{SM}."

Confucius once said that, "All wisdom begins with the proper naming of things," or "The Rectification of Names".

For example, I could never be satisfied in producing something called a town or community video. This gross under-positioning sounds as though it is one step removed from homespun two-minute videos posted on YouTube from a family barbecue or outing.

Notice how PBS doesn't call their show *State Videos* but rather, *Aerial America*. They do so because they understand branding. Sadly, most in our Industry do not. Thus, we are left with, "I did a town video!"

This is why Larry Vecchio, Co-founder of Town-Advisor, and I presently produce *Real Estate Town Docu-Mentaries^{SM}*. Check out the difference, and you will see how we have elevated the meaning of the towns and cities that folks call home. *(http://townadvisor.info/documentaries)*

"Since Residents are interested in both their town and Real Estate... I combined the two!"

For this same reason, I selected the name Real Estate Town Meetings^{SM}, as it signals something of far greater importance to the entire town; more than a local company doing a buyer's night.

Each Real Estate Town Meeting^{SM} I set up (which I will go into greater detail about in our *Certified Community Marketing Specialist^{SM}* online course) literally led to a hundred, or at times hundreds, of local residents turning out.

The Real Estate Town Meeting^{SM} was about everything to do with Real Estate in that town; a subject which homeowners cannot resist.

I wasn't looking for "buyers" but homesellers... whom I attracted, whom then became buyers.

I hope this small taste of four community-based ideas makes a difference in your company's strategy towards *Creating Real Estate Connections* within your communities.

Oh, and one last point about larger community communication. You should not have your Associates say, "I work out of the Pleasanton office." When asked where they work, they should say, "I work out of the (county/town name) Regional Sales and Marketing Center." Otherwise, if a consumer lives two towns away, they might conclude that they should not list their home with your Associate... since that office is actually defining a competitive town to where they live.

Chapter 9

Creating Connections with Out-of-State Buyers and Sellers

by Pam Charron
Exclusive TownAdvisor Member for
Sarasota, Bradenton, Venice, Longboat Key, and Lakewood Ranch, Florida

Pam Charron:

Born and raised in New England, Pam started college with the intent of becoming a paralegal, and then a lawyer. In 1981 she was hired to work in her family-owned business where it quickly became apparent that Pam had a natural sales ability. It is here she met her husband of many years and where she remained as a top inside sales person for the company, Charron Incorporated, until it was sold in the early 2000s. Pam took her 20+ years of marketing, business management and sales experience to her second career as a Realtor® with Prudential Verani in New Hampshire, soaring to their top agent after her first full year in real estate. Moving to Sarasota, Florida in 2007, she continued her quest to be the best she could be by assisting homeowners and homebuyers in maximizing their real estate investments. Working with Berkshire Hathaway HomeServices Florida Realty, Pam is consistently rated in the top 1% of Realtors® in her market area. In her spare time, Pam enjoys reading, boating and spending time with her husband, David and their two cats, Max and Lacy.

Favorite Quote:

"Quality is never an accident; it is always the result of high intention, sincere effort and skillful execution." – Will A. Foster

---

I was recently quoted in an area magazine as stating, "I like to consider myself not only a Realtor® but an 'area advisor'." Thus, this chapter's topic is quite appropriate. Then, let me first share a little about my background and how I've grown my business exponentially through a community-centric approach, versus an agent-centric approach.

Originally from New Hampshire, my husband and I owned a nationally recognized lighting agency which served ME, NH, and VT a business started by my father-in-law, and still recognized today. Since most of my clients were not located in my town, I learned the importance of service- excellence, long distance relationship-building and, also, following my father-in-law's worthy advice "... that I did not need to know every answer; I just needed to know how to find the answer," advice I still follow today.

Coming from a close family of eight, it was a difficult time when my father fell gravely ill at the age of 67. I visited him each of his last 47 days in the hospital, and spent hours reminiscing, sharing our victories, our struggles and some tears. The most poignant and profound, life-changing moment for me was when my Dad looked at me and said, "Pam, if there is anything else in life you want to do, do it now; as you will be here someday. It happens sooner than you think." That is how I chose the path of real estate as my second career, a career as equally-fulfilling as my first.

As a successful Realtor® in New Hampshire, I relocated my business to Sarasota at the end of 2007. This was a time when our housing market was falling rapidly into deep distress, with no immediate relief in sight. I didn't know one soul in Sarasota, and had only visited this special city over two weekends. It was clear that most people thought I was crazy.

How could I build a business in a town I didn't know, with no contacts in real estate, in "the Great Recession" and Florida housing bust? But, I did just that. Since I had just gone through the evaluation process of several locations where "winter is no more," I had first-hand experience on how important it is to be able to learn about the "community" before selecting a home; and how the information I needed to make an informed decision was not easy to come by. I wanted to make this relocation-relevant information a priority and available when serving my future clients.

The first thing I did was to find a civics course (and now my husband thought I was crazy). I spent six weeks, which included evening classes and day trips, learning all about the area that I chose to live in. I joined the Chamber of Commerce, visited many open houses, attended classes at our Realtor® Association, toured communities and visited membership clubs. Of course, I also found a few of my favorite community causes to support locally. Thankfully, after hard work and dedication, in only a few short years, I had a thriving career and I am certain that my attitude of being an ambassador for my town and a servant to my customers, was a prime contributor to my success.

"TownAdvisor Real Estate Town Docu-Mentaries℠ set both me and my communities apart."

The absence of local relationships caused me to focus heavily on building my Realtor® referral network within the pockets of feeder-markets and my home state. I tapped into both by determining who owns property in Sarasota that also owns property in other areas. Through direct-mail, agent-to-agent contact, and the direct promotion of my TownAdvisor site, I am recognized as the trusted go-to person for Sarasota. Commonly, when a Realtor® in another area is looking to assist their client with a real estate purchase out of their area, they want to be sure they find the perfect Realtor®, since that referral will directly reflect on them… good or bad. Through the internet, agents will commonly look for a Realtor® who shares the same professional designation as they do,

105

such as CCMS (Certified Community Marketing Specialist*SM*)... someone who exemplifies superior knowledge of their community and success in the industry.

So many couples, families and retirees dream of either moving to Florida, or having a second home where they can escape the dark, cold winters of the north. As I meet people, whether by referral or simply an inquiry from my website, I ask them to share their current lifestyle and what community features are important to them. I listen intently. Our initial dialogue is about their visions and dreams, versus how many bedrooms and baths they need. Are they golfers or boaters? Like strolling the beach or biking? Do they have children and require school information? How do they see themselves living in Florida and have they ever visited the Gulf Coast? The reaction is always positive and they feel more at ease knowing that I take a specific interest in their lifestyle, versus just selling them a house.

Of course, we eventually get to their specific housing requirements and desired price point, but having the idea of how they see themselves within a community allows me to narrow down neighborhoods and make their visits more productive. That is why, once I have an out-of-state buyer's email address, I immediately send them the link to my Real Estate Town Docu-Mentary*SM* (which is also proudly displayed on my website), so they can see how I am showcasing the value of living in Sarasota. It also clearly shows that I am an area expert by providing valuable information about the area they may invest in. Further, being an interactive site, prospective buyers can enjoy the community reviews posted by people from around the world. Could there be any better endorsement of an area?

Moving to a new location, although exciting, can be quite stressful. Often, those new to the area "don't know what they don't know" and yearn for the knowledge to make an informed decision. I recognize my clients' time is valuable. I want each visitor to know that I take pride in where I live, and am happy to share everything I know about my town, or direct them to where they can find additional answers.

I keep a supply of print material, maps, resource websites and service-providers on hand. I realize that there are times when my community may not be the perfect fit. My clients still deserve the time and attention it takes to assist them in arriving at their personal relocation decision. Those whom you fervently assist will become your advocates, which just might result in future business. And, if not, I have represented the town that I love, proudly.

My business is largely working with Sellers who own property here in Sarasota and elsewhere, some of whom I will never meet in person. (Think about developing a relationship of trust with someone you will never meet.) Whether the Seller is an investor, a snowbird, or the recipient of an estate property, it is imperative that, rather than just promoting myself and my accomplishments, I demonstrate how worthy I am of representing one of their most valuable assets. We have all heard that a Buyer forms an opinion of a property in the first 15 seconds. I keep this in the back of my mind every time I speak to a new Seller. A simple Google search of my name will let the prospective Seller know that I am tech savvy, successful and a community advocate worthy of selling Sarasota above all other areas of Florida. My advice to anyone who primarily works with out-of-state clients is to have in-depth knowledge of your community and let the world know it!

My best marketing idea for out-of-state homeowners is my Sarasota Real Estate Town Docu-Mentary^SM. In ten minutes, there's nothing I could possibly do that could ever compete with how this program convinces out-of-state homeowners that nobody markets where their property is located, Greater Sarasota, like I do. I also feature my Real Esatte Town Docu-Mentary^SM at the Sarasota Airport.

These out-of-state owners, many of whom live in the Northeast, are direct, to-the-point, don't want to hear any fluff, and aren't interested in personal promotion... but they are all interested in how I'll promote the value of what they own, and nothing has ever convinced them like this community video I mail to them on my personal and market-area flashdrive, along with the link to my Sarasota TownAdvisor website.

I'm often told that my enthusiasm is infectious. I believe that is true, but I also know it is genuine. Taking pride in your community, staying on top of current events, knowing economic statistics and being able to connect your neighbors with others (including businesses) will help you shine above the rest. It is never about me, but always about the client. Yes, as a Realtor®, I still feel it is important to keep a strong presence via social media and partake in conventional marketing methods, but there is no doubt that the success I have experienced as a Real Estate Professional (both in New Hampshire and in Florida) is due to my commitment to the town I live in. Love what you do and do it well.

Dalton's Take-away:

Pam exemplifies how a winner in Real Estate can migrate to a new area, start their Real Estate business anew, and (within a several month period) be out in front of all local Realtors® who have spent their entire lives in that region... by promoting the benefits of living within her new community.

Chapter 10

<u>Serving the Celebrity Community</u>
an interview with Valerie Fitzgerald

by Allan Dalton

Valerie Fitzgerald:

Valerie, although not one to draw attention to her accomplishments, has effectively transacted approximately $2 Billion worth of greater Los Angeles Real Estate. Valerie is the President of the preeminent Valerie Fitzgerald Group, part of the Beverly Hills Coldwell Banker Real Estate Firm. Valerie was cited by the Los Angeles Business Journal for achieving the highest sales volume in Los Angeles County for Residential Real Estate. Her best-selling book *Heart and Sold: How to Survive and Build a Recession-Proof Business* has also contributed to her being recognized as one of the Real Estate Industries most important voices. Valerie's highly credible and charismatic television presence also significantly contributed to the HGTV hit "Selling LA."

<u>Favorite Quote(s)</u>:

"I dwell in possibility." – Emily Dickinson

Allan Dalton:

Since Beverly Hills and Valerie Fitzgerald are synonymous with celebrityhood, I believe, who better than you, Valerie – given your illustrious and luminary-led marketplace – to speak to the subject of serving the celebrity community.

Valerie Fitzgerald:

Thank you, Allan. Although I must say that I view all of my clients as deserving celebrity-like care and treatment, I also recognize that I am very fortunate to represent a significant percentage of so-called "A-listers." I also would like to point out that my market extends well beyond Beverly Hills, as I cover much of West Los Angeles and many other segments of Southern California.

A. Dalton:

Valerie, since you are known throughout the industry for your legendary commitment to superior representation for your valued and varied clients from all backgrounds and pedigrees, it comes as no surprise to me that you would want to make the distinction that you, and your highly accomplished Team of Professionals, treat all of your clients with the highest level of possible professionalism. That said, as one who perhaps (as much as any other Realtor® in America is known for serving world-renowned clients), what can you tell our readers regarding this particularly prestigious and celebrated community?

109

V. Fitzgerald:

Allan, this may be the briefest chapter in your book as, for starters, I never publicly divulge the names of any of my clients (unless they have asked me to) and, considering how all of my so-called "Celebrity Clients" painstakingly seek to preserve their privacy, I won't be dropping any names for your book on *Creating Real Estate Connections.*

A. Dalton:

Well, why don't we just have you address some of the general rules that you follow... and we'll leave it at that?

V. Fitzgerald:

Fine. Here is my philosophy and practices for serving the needs of what others refer to as "the very rich and very famous":
1. Complete confidentiality
2. No generic and personal prospecting... all initial contact must be managed through privileged networking
3. Ego-less presentations
4. Substantiate all recommendations
5. Serve both the client and their Advisory Teams

A. Dalton:

Great, Valerie. Let's take them one at a time... starting with "Complete Confidentiality."

V. Fitzgerald:

Allan, since it's a given that this caliber of client, often times, is being "virtually stalked" regarding where they might be moving to next, I always make it a point to be the first person who stresses that all of their personal and professional dealings with me, and my accomplished staff, will remain completely confidential... well beyond the transaction itself.

This is no small point as, if the prospective client brings it up first, they, of course, expect that I would agree. But, by me taking the initiative and addressing this all-important subject first, it introduces high credibility and offers greater assurance.

A. Dalton:

Valerie, what do you mean when you say, "No Generic and Personal Prospecting?"

V. Fitzgerald:

What I mean, Allan, is that (ironically) if it appears to certain people within the celebrity community that I need to prospect aggressively for their business, it conveys the impression that either I am fighting too hard or that important people, like themselves, are not inclined to recommend me. It can actually hurt my chances if my first point of contact isn't managed properly.

A. Dalton:
What about the "Ego-less Presentations"?

V. Fitzgerald:
The level of notoriety and acclaim that my most illustrious clients command, means that they are not accustomed to other individuals honoring their own achievements in their presence. Accordingly, it would be unseemly for me to hold these prospective clients hostage while they first had to learn of my so-called "Real Estate stardom" as a precursor to working together.

A. Dalton:
Valerie, I'm interested to hear your response to your 4th rule... that you "Substantiate all Recommendations."

V. Fitzgerald:
There is a general suspicion among many of the world's most celebrated citizens, especially in the entertainment field, that they must be very cautious of any financial-related advice. Many so-called stars (although I represent many CEOs as well), know of personal friends who are presently suffering through making disastrous financial decisions with those they should never have trusted.

111

Therefore, the more I back up all that I purport to be true, the greater the confidence level I create among these clients and, equally importantly, their Advisory Teams. Many of my clients have Business Managers and Financial Teams who are completely involved in their Real Estate decisions.

Given the professional backgrounds of their Advisors (be they Attorneys, Tax Attorneys, CPAs, and Certified Financial Planners), it is not surprising that their approach to Real Estate decision-making is far more analytical and thorough. Many of these Advisors seek to protect their clients from making overly emotional decisions.

I should also point out, Allan, that (although many of these celebrities enjoy enormous wealth), their incomes are quite sporadic. For example, some of my clients may make $10 million dollars... and then no money for the two following years. This means that *my Team* must work with *their Team* in securing customized financing.

A. Dalton:
Well, Valerie, you've done a great job of walking the fine line between not dropping names but dropping a tremendous game-plan to working within the Celebrity Community. Is there anything you would like to say in closing?

V. Fitzgerald:
I don't think I would be the Realtor® I am today, nor would my Team of colleagues be as accomplished as they are, if a major part of our DNA was not comprised of years of working with a caliber of clients who truly demand the very best, along with their Team of Advisors. I can say, without any reservation, that I treat all of my clients as the most important people in the world and what has helped me is to learn from professionals in many other related businesses and industries regarding the importance of skills, and high-level service.

A. Dalton:
Thank you very much, Valerie, for contributing to *Creating Real Estate Connections.*

V. Fitzgerald:
Allan, how could I say, "no," considering the personal contribution you made to my book, *Heart and Sold: How to Survive and Build a Recession-Proof Business.*

Dalton's Take-away:

The way in which Valerie describes building a sacred trust with her celebrity clients should serve as a blueprint for how every Real Estate client in the world should be honored.

Chapter 11

When Community Properties Become Distressed
an interview with Brandon Brittingham

by Gee Dunsten

Brandon Brittingham:

Brandon Brittingham of Long and Foster companies is recognized as one of the top Real Estate Agents in the country and has garnered national attention for his production and the awards he has received in a short time in the industry. In 2012 Brandon was named one of the Top 30 Realtors® under 30 by the National Associations of Realtors®.

Brandon was ranked in the Top 250 Agents in the Nation by The Wall Street Journal and Real Trends in both 2012-2013 with over 33 million in sales over 266 transactions. Brandon, who recently formed the Maryland and Delaware Group of Long and Foster along with his partner Doug Gardiner, manages 18 agents that serve a wide market in Maryland, both on the Eastern and Western Shore.

Brandon is known for his cutting-edge marketing both online and offline, employing professional video and photographs for his listings and was recently named 2014 Coastal Associations of Realtors® Realtor® of the Year.

Brandon has earned the top producer award on the Eastern Shore four years in a row and had the number one team on the eastern shore with volume and units in 2013. Also known as an advocate for his community giving by awarding the "Brandon Brittingham Scholarship" every year and working with various boards and community groups to enhance his local community.

Favorite Quote:

"It is not the beauty of a building you should look at; it's the construction of the foundation that will stand the test of time."   – David Allan Coe

---

Gee Dunsten:
Brandon, when did you get into the real estate business?

Brandon Brittingham:
I started about 6 years ago. My father and grandfather were home builders here on the Eastern Shore of Maryland, so it seemed like a good fit.

G. Dunten:
Why did you enter the distressed property market?

B. Brittingham:
At the time I was getting started, there was already an established core of experienced agents that dominated most of the market. The economy, as well as our real estate business, was in decline. I could see the handwriting on the wall...people struggling to make their house payments, property values going down. The distressed property segment was going to be huge. And, there was less than a handful of local agents

114

actually involved in that segment. When I asked agents in my office why they weren't doing any short sales, they would roll their eyes and share the same resounding answer, "They take too much time – and most of the time – they never get done!"

G. Dunsten:
How big did the distressed market actually become in your town?

B. Brittingham:
Between 40 and 45% and in some price ranges, 50 to 60%. It's still between 25 and 30%. In fact, Maryland has recently surpassed Florida and is now ranked as the number one state for distressed properties in the country.

G. Dunsten:
What did you discover after you jumped into REOs and short sales, Brandon?

B. Brittingham:
It became clear that there was very little being taught about distressed properties. Most real estate agents, companies, and even lenders were flying by the seat of their pants. The entire country, from Wall Street to Banking, to the Government, was in denial about how bad things were. The Industry wasn't prepared for the tidal wave of distressed properties forming offshore. There was lots of abuse, due to a lack of regulations and procedures. It was like the Wild, Wild West. Organizations, businesses, and individuals were doing whatever they wanted. I've always had a thirst for knowledge and there weren't any mentors, so I had to become self-educated. I attended every meeting, workshop, conference, and seminar that came along and asked lots of questions and interviewed lots of people who seemed to be successful. I read anything and everything I could find online and offline... including the amazing Four Rs of Short Sales by Allan Dalton.

G. Dunsten:
What are some of the benefits of doing short sales and/or REO's?

B. Brittingham:
There are four major benefits:
  1. On a national level, distressed properties represent between 10 and 11% of the residential housing market.
  2. There is not much competition.
  3. You create raving fans. When you save someone from losing their home to foreclosure, they never forget you.
  4. It's also good for your community, county, state, and nation.

G. Dunsten:

Brandon, you've done hundreds of REO's and short sales. What are some of your keys to success?

B. Brittingham:

Gee, there are a number of things. You must be:

1. System-oriented
2. Good in dealing with time controls where there isn't any flexibility in deadlines
3. A good listener, as well as a good communicator
4. Willing to put your ego aside, because it's not about you
5. Passionate about helping people
6. Relentless to get the job done
7. A fair, but firm negotiator
8. Able to handle challenges with a "no big deal" attitude
9. Committed to keeping up-to-date - (Procedures will continue to change.), and
10. Thoroughly providing people with all of the relevant distressed property options not just the REO and short sale outcome.

In addition, you must recognize that:

1. Procedures are critical
2. There is a lot of paperwork that must be micro-managed and exact
3. You will need to have a good working knowledge of the different requirements and procedures from lender to lender and investor to investor (Fannie Mae, FHA, etc.)

G. Dunsten:

How hard is it to get into the REO side of the distressed property business?

B. Brittingham:

The entry is very difficult, because most of the lenders have already established long-term relationships with a real estate broker or agent. It takes a major commitment of time, energy, and expense to build your REO business. You must do extra relevant things for the lender over time to prove your value. Each lender/bank has their own procedures and asset managers, so it starts with getting your foot in the door by going above and beyond what's required. You must provide a tireless attitude, extra effort, and a reputation for outstanding performance on each task/job.

You must also convince lenders that you are 100% committed to protecting and preserving their assets, to the degree possible, as opposed to being seen as an opportunist.

G. Dunsten:
What's the biggest challenge with REOs?

B. Brittingham:
There are really two main challenges, Gee. First, they are labor-intensive. Most agents who aren't involved with them don't realize the amount of work that is required for each property. It takes effort, time, and the ability to handle lots of pressure. The demands and expectations from the bank are enormous. You can't afford to make a mistake. There is no forgiveness, because there are another 100 good agents that the bank can give their business to. REO agents must babysit the property, making weekly visits, providing written reports, and often dealing with maintenance issues.

The second challenge involves working with the co-op agents and their lack of knowledge and experience. They:
1. Don't understand how the process works... like many, they all want success but they don't want to become educated
2. Want to amend the "bank's contract"
3. Want to verbally negotiate
4. Don't follow procedures or adhere to the timeline

The REO agent must possess a hunger to do well and be 100% committed to representing their client successfully through the transaction.

G. Dunsten:
This segment of our business is clearly a lot of work, Brandon. What are the benefits?

B. Brittingham:
It's a huge opportunity to get into the "investor world." Lots of REO properties are bought by investors. It opens lots of doors. The more REO's you are involved with, the more investors will come directly to you. Investors quickly recognize who has REO's to sell. They are always proactively looking for deals.

G. Dunsten:
Where's a good place to start?

B. Brittingham:
Start by building your local connections with banks, attorneys, and financial planners. They're in the community and so are you! At the end of the day, you must form relationships, so join organizations and participate on committees where people can get to know you in a non-real estate environment. You want to be known as a good thinker, hard

worker, and enthusiastic community member which will build those bridges that will open future doors to real estate discussions.

G. Dunsten:
In other words, you must endeavor to be viewed as a professional contemporary. How important is the short sale segment?

B. Brittingham:
Short sales are bigger nationwide than REO's and there is less competition.

G. Dunsten:
How are short sales different from REO's?

B. Brittingham:
In an REO, you are working with the bank, which enables you to have direct communication with the bank/seller. They have terms and a price already in mind, as well as a timeline by which they want to dispose of the property. In a short sale, you are dealing with the seller, the lender, and the investor, all with their own agendas. While the process has become more efficient, it can still take several months for all the parties to reach an agreement and the transaction to go through. There is a much greater chance of some unforeseen issue or problem popping up that you'll have to deal with. It's like playing Whack-a-Mole. Every time an obstacle pops up, you've got to deal with it and knock it back down to keep the whole process from derailing.

G. Dunsten:
What is the biggest challenge in working with short sales?

B. Brittingham:
The biggest challenge with short sales is that you get one bank's process figured out and the next time, they change it. Every successful short sale starts with having a good candidate, because short sales were never intended to be a "get out of mortgage free card," although over the years, lenders have been less rigid and more flexible when evaluating the short sale homeowner.

G. Dunsten:
Brandon, what are the most critical steps to having a successful short sale?

B. Brittingham:
Gee, there are six critical steps:
   1. Qualifying the homeowner

118

There are four qualifications for a short sale:
  a) Need to sell
  b) An acceptable hardship has occurred since they took out the loan which prevents them from paying their mortgage obligation
  c) No assets to pay off the loan
  d) Must have or will soon have a financial shortfall

We start with an extensive phone interview prior to our first face-to-face meeting, because if they aren't qualified, there is no reason to get together. I use a Seller Questionnaire consisting of 27 questions.

Seller Questionnaire:
  1) Is your property currently for sale on the market? Is it listed with a Real Estate agent/brokerage?
  2) When was the property purchased?
  3) What was the original purchase price?
  4) Who is on the title (deed) for the property?
  5) Who is on the mortgage?
  6) What kind of mortgage do you have (conventional, VA, FHA)?
  7) How many mortgages do you have?
  8) Do you have any HELOCs (Home Equity Line of Credit)?
  9) Who is/are your lender(s)?
  10) Do you have mortgage insurance?
  11) Are you living in the property? If not, where are you living and is the property being maintained?
  12) What is the condition of the property?
  13) If relocating, how soon do you have to move?
  14) How much do you owe, approximately?
  15) Are you current on your HOA or condo payments?
  16) Do you owe back taxes or are there any liens on your property?
  17) Have you considered or are you considering declaring bankruptcy?
  18) Are you current on all mortgage payments and will you be able to remain current?
  19) What lender correspondence/notifications have you received?
  20) Do you have assets that will allow you to pay down your mortgage?
  21) What is the situation that caused you to miss or will cause you to miss making your payments?
  22) If no payments have been missed, why do you need to sell?
  23) What are your current monthly payments, including taxes and insurance?
  24) How much money are you currently earning?

25) What are your estimated monthly expenses?
26) Do you hold any kind of security clearance?
27) Are you considering a loan modification?

2. Send prospective clients to a CPA and an attorney.
Before you start the short sale process with any client, I strongly advise you to send them to a CPA. Short sales can have complicated tax ramifications and the seller needs professional advice prior to moving forward. As real estate agents, we cannot give this kind of advice. An attorney may be needed in certain situations, and will always be needed when it comes time to interpret the approval letter.

Some situations are so complex because of other liens/debt, that they may need to be negotiated by an attorney. The seller will need legal advice prior to moving forward with the short sale. I always advise them to speak to an attorney, regardless of the type of transaction.

3. Getting a title search and pulling the deed before starting the short sale process.
I cannot stress enough that you must do a title search prior to doing a short sale and you absolutely have to pull the deed prior to moving forward on the sale.

There is a good chance that if the buyers have not been current on their mortgage they could be behind on other credit, as well and a lien could be filed on the house. If the property is in an HOA or has a condo association, you should verify whether or not the HOA is up to date. I have heard and seen many horror stories, where agents get a short sale approval only to find out that there is a problem title and they cannot go to settlement. As I've already said, another extremely important initial step is to pull the actual deed to the property. That way you can verify who is listed on the deed and that you are dealing with all parties involved.

I have seen several family issues and divorce issues where one party tried to sell the home without letting the other party know.

4. Determining the loan type.

Determining the seller's loan type is a very important step and should be done at the very beginning. It should be done in tandem with assembling the package, and you need to know exactly what procedure and guidelines you are to follow.

Knowing the loan type can help you determine exactly which process to follow during the short sale process, and it saves you a lot of time and energy. Finding out the type of loan is relatively simple and can usually be determined by simply looking at the seller's last payment statement. You can check to see if a property is Fannie/Freddie owned by going on their respective websites. Some examples of different loan types are:

1) FHA
2) VA
3) HAFA
4) Fannie/Freddie-backed traditional short sale (non-HAFA)
5) Portfolio loans

5. The package.

One of the most important parts of being successful in a short sale transaction is making sure that you have a COMPLETE AND ACCURATE package. Most short sales get delayed because of an incomplete or inaccurate package. This applies to not only what is required by the bank, but to forms that protect you from a liability standpoint, to any information that will help you get your short sale accepted. You need to submit a stellar package to differentiate yours from the other 300 that are sitting on the negotiator's desk. Think of yourself as an attorney who is defending a client. In order to do your job properly, you have to provide as much conclusive evidence as possible to support your case. You should acquire any and all information that will help to strengthen your case. You can find out exactly what each lender requires in a package submitted to them by visiting their website.

6. Maintaining constant communication with all parties to the transaction, including the lender, while monitoring the process and timelines.

G. Dunsten:
Do you have any closing thoughts you'd like to share, Brandon?

B. Brittingham:
Working in the short sale market takes lots of energy, time, patience, control, and fortitude, however, the rewards can be great. There's nothing more satisfying than preventing a family who is going through difficult circumstances from facing eviction.

Instead of losing their home to foreclosure, you've enabled them to relocate with dignity and less damage to their credit. In addition, you've assisted their neighbors in maintaining a higher property value.

Dalton's Take-away:

After reading Gee's interview with Brandon, I can now understand why Gee Dunsten (President of our Certified Community Marketing Specialist designation course) has invited (and Brandon has accepted) Brandon to lead our efforts in making Distressed Property Management as one of the many modules that will be comprised in this online certification program.

Having access to Brandon, in our interactive format, will be invaluable; along with our other faculty members (as well as those not included in this book).

Chapter 12

Strategically and Sensitively Serving Seniors
an interview with John Riggins

by Gee Dunsten

John Riggins:

After serving his country as a US Army airborne ranger in Vietnam, John (now of John Riggins Real Estate) was transferred to Hawaii and fell in love with the state and its people. It was then John resigned his commission and entered the Real Estate business. Since that time, John has helped over 3000 families buy and sell homes, aided countless homeowners with loan modifications, and expedited more than 550 short sales.

John has been working daily in Hawaii residential Real Estate since 1977, acquiring knowledge, skill, and experience that he imparts to his team which assists buyers and sellers over several different time zones from the US east coast to the Philippines. John is very proud to have been named one of the top 50 Realtors in North America by Howard Brinton and Bill Barrett.

Favorite Quote:

"You may never be financially rich, however if you are always honest and treat people the way you would want to be treated, you'll always be rich in friends." – John's Grandmother

Gee Dunsten:

John, when did you get into the real estate business?

John Riggins:

Gee, I started taking real estate classes in 1976. In those days, Hawaii only offered the real estate exam a couple of times each year. Because the exam was sent to Princeton, NJ for processing, it took another 2-3 months to get your license, which for me, was Jan. 4, 1977. We didn't have any GRI or CRS classes back then. Fortunately, I got great training from a number of top brokers who took a personal interest in helping to prepare me to succeed! As a result, I have always had a thirst for knowledge. Most people today who enter our business aren't thinking about getting educated. Their main focus is doing deals and getting a higher commission split. Getting educated, staying educated, and networking with other top producers around the country has been the backbone of my success.

G. Dunsten:

What percentage of your business comes from Seniors?

J. Riggins:

It's big. The overwhelming majority of my business comes from Baby Boomers/Seniors. I work almost exclusively with them, while my son picks up a bigger percentage of the younger market, although he just got a referral from a landscaper for a 925K listing from a little old retired lady who is moving to Colorado.

G. Dunsten:
What caused your shift in working primarily with senior clients?

J. Riggins:
Gee, it's like this. Someone buys a new Honda automobile and then begins to notice how many other people are driving Hondas. I'm 71 years old and will soon turn 72. As I've gotten older I've gravitated towards working with my chronological contemporaries because I am one of them, and they've gravitated to me for the same reason. Our senior market is already big. People live longer in Hawaii than in any other state in the country. Most Seniors are still active, perhaps because of our wonderful weather, happier environment, and great places to walk and swim. In fact, the state of Hawaii is expecting exponential growth in the senior market between 2015 and 2030. The demand for more universal products and services is also growing. While some states like Florida, Texas, and Delaware don't have any state income tax, in Hawaii lots of our citizens have Federal and military pensions which also are not subject to tax.

G. Dunsten:
With all of these benefits are there any disadvantages to living on one of your eight islands?

J. Riggins:
Unfortunately, yes.

1. Our homes and living expenses are high, especially for those who are on a fixed income. In fact, we refer to Las Vegas as Hawaii's ninth island, because many Seniors who can no longer afford our high cost of living, are moving to Las Vegas for its warm climate and lower cost of living.

2. Distance – It's a five-hour flight to the mainland.

3. Fewer single-level homes – Most of our vacant land is either owned by the local, State, or Federal government and this creates a shortage of suitable building lots. Builders just aren't building single-level homes. The vast majority are condos or two-story homes that don't even have a first-floor master bedroom. The shortage of inventory and increase in demand often causes our single-level homes to sell for more than the asking price.

G. Dunsten:
John, what are some of the differences in working with Seniors?

J. Riggins:

Well Gee, the majority of Seniors would like to work with an older agent and there are several things to keep in mind. You must be:

1. More patient
2. Prepared to arrive early or at least, on time
3. Well-dressed and well-groomed
4. Courteous and polite - (Seniors expect good old-fashioned manners!)
5. A good listener
6. Prepared to spend extra time on every appointment/visit – (I plan on at least 3 hours to socialize and answer any questions they might have.)

In addition, you should know that:

1. Many Seniors have difficulty reading small print, so all of your materials, including documents and Agreements/Contracts must have a bigger font.
2. Most Seniors prefer to meet face-to-face.
3. For many Seniors, their hearing is a challenge, so you should sit face-to-face with your decision-makers. I always strongly suggest that we sit at their kitchen table directly across from each other, so they can hear and see everything that I am talking about.
4. Since many Seniors are not electronically-oriented, you must be able to offer other delivery systems.
5. Seniors want to explore all of their options from downsizing, to senior communities, to Assisted Living. Your local knowledge is critical and you must be willing to invest your time in helping them explore their options.
6. Seniors are usually slow to make decisions.
7. Often, Seniors have grown kids or grandchildren who are involved as advisors.
8. You must be knowledgeable about the different types of reversed mortgage financing, such as lump sum, monthly draw, and line of credit, etc.

G. Dunsten:

What are most Seniors looking for in their next home, John?

126

J. Riggins:

If they are buying, it's because they want to downsize. Some of the features they are looking for are:

1. One level
2. Wider doors
3. Accessible shower or walk-in tub
4. Lower sinks, countertops, and cabinets
5. Better lighting, especially in the kitchen and bathrooms
6. Grab bars in the bathrooms
7. Low maintenance
8. Yard maintenance
9. Energy efficiency – (Remember, most Seniors are on a fixed income).
10. Safety
11. Nearby conveniences
12. Walkable communities – (Close to doctor, pharmacy, grocery store, restaurants, etc. – Very popular in Hawaii)
13. Turn-key – (Most Seniors don't want to be involved in a makeover or rehab.)
14. Close distance to hospital

In addition, Seniors will carefully examine all kinds of fees, such as HOA/condo, maintenance, water and sewer, power expenses, and trash collection.

G. Dunsten:

Do you have any other thoughts or suggestions?

J. Riggins:

Yes, Gee, I do. Most Seniors, who also have a house to sell, usually fall into two types of categories. Some are hoarders, so you must be very sensitive and careful in how you deal with their challenges, such as suggesting that Martha take down her treasured velvet Elvis picture from about its revered spot over the fireplace. For others, their home is in good condition, but dated, so any updates or makeovers become a big issue.

Because they sometimes lack experience and/or imagination, virtual staging can be an effective tool in helping them visualize and better understand how certain changes can make the house more marketable to younger buyers.

You should also be prepared for other influencers, such as grown children, a confidential friend, an attorney, and/or a CPA, to be involved.

Often you will be called upon to do other things for your senior clients beyond your Realtor® responsibilities, such as drive them to the doctor or grocery store, because their children are not available. Going the extra mile not only enhances your relationship, it often generates more senior client business from other Seniors who have heard about how great you are in looking out for your clients' best interests and welfare.

G. Dunsten:

John, do you have any tips on how some of our readers can grow their Senior business?

J. Riggins:

1. Take a couple of SRES (Senior Real Estate Specialist) classes from NAR®. They are essential. In fact, I'm taking their Universal Design for Accessibility class next month.

2. Visit or volunteer at places where Seniors like to participate, such as golf courses, community centers, places of worship, Senior social clubs/organizations, service organizations, and local hospitals.

3. Offer to teach classes on downsizing or how to retrofit your present home.

4. Develop a monthly, direct mail program with jumbo-sized postcards consisting of six holiday cards, as well as homeownership tips, Just Sold and Just Listed announcements.

5. Set aside at least a couple of hours per week to make 2-3 minute calls to past clients, neighbors, and friends. "I was just driving through your neighborhood and I thought of you, ____. How are you and ____ doing?" or "I'm between appointments and just wanted to check in with you. How is ____? Doing okay?" Seniors love to hear from you!

6. Drop off or send annual calendars filled with wonderful photos of your area.

7. Don't be afraid to spend some time with them.

8. Remember, the more Seniors you help, the more friends they'll send your way.

G. Dunsten:

Any closing thoughts, John?

J. Riggins:

My grandmother used to say, "John, always be honest with people. Do the very best for them and you will always have friends." Stay true to your core values and help others.

Images from John's beloved Honolulu: The city itself and the King Kamehameha statue.

Dalton's Take-Away:

While the Rolling Stones memorialized the lyrics, "What a drag it is getting old," such dire words do not apply to those fortunate enough to both live in Hawaii and be served by the greatness and sensitivity of John Riggins.

Chapter 13

Military Clients - How to Best Serve Those Who have Served
an interview with Alexis Bolin

by Gee Dunsten

Alexis Bolin:

Alexis with ERA Legacy Realty has been in Real Estate for the past 36 years with ERA Real Estate, has been ERA's #1 Nationwide Agent three times, and is currently ranked in the Top 10 for ERA Agents in the nation. Inducted into the Real Estate Experts Hall of Fame in August 2012, she was also named one of the Top 25 Most Powerful Women in NW Florida by Climate Magazine. Alexis, with over 4000 closed residential real estate transaction in her career, is a popular speaker, panelist and moderator.

<u>Favorite Quote(s)</u>:

"Don't get so high that you forget where you come from. You are not put on this earth to mark time. You are put here to make a difference in someone else's life."   – Rachel Barshafsky
(Alexis' grandmother)

A. Bolin:

The Military Community is very loyal. It is a case of, "If you have my back, I'll have yours." The military looks for someone who has walked in their shoes, someone who really has their best interest at heart – as well as their family's. You really need to know that they often have a very limited time to find and buy a house. They want all the data they can gather about housing alternatives, the area, lifestyle, community, hospitals, schools, and more. They are looking for someone who can guide them through the entire process. Someone who will also help prevent them from stepping on an alligator!

G. Dunsten:

How do you go about meeting this big challenge?

A. Bolin:

I tell them from the beginning: "Your job is to find the house. You pick the home. I don't because I'm not going to be living there. My job is to help put your family in a neighborhood where you will be comfortable, with schools that meet the challenges required by your children, and where you will feel safe." You must be able to tell them you can relate to walking in their shoes. It's so much easier when you can relate to them and their situation.

G. Dunsten:

What are some of the key areas that you must pay special attention to?

A. Bolin:

Well, Gee it starts with the military spouse. Their main job is to support their active duty spouse and to take away some of their stress. It's the agent's job to make the home-buying process as less stressful as possible. Most of these families move every 3 years. Often all or most of the family members don't want to leave where they are, so the move is that much more stressful on everyone. Plus, they must be able to fit into their new community, so the pressure is on for them to find the right person to introduce them to all facets of Pensacola. You must possess an extensive knowledge of your community because most of these families are arriving here for the first time. It's very important to allocate enough time to tour anything and everything that is or will be important about where they want to live, as well as what type of house they want to live in.

G. Dunsten:

So, Alexis, what types of things are included in your client tour?

A. Bolin:

Gee, we always tour the Base. I want them to know where their spouse will be working, as well as where things are located, like the Base Hospital, Commissary, Officers' Club or NCO Club, and recreational facilities. Like any out-of-town buyer and/or relocation candidate, we also do an extensive tour of downtown, highlighting some of our numerous landmarks, shopping areas, parks and recreation, etc. In addition, we tour a variety of neighborhoods based on their wants, needs, and budget.

G. Dunsten:

Because the Navy is a major employer in Pensacola, what role does the Board of Realtors® play?

A. Bolin:

Our Board has a group that volunteers to work with the Navy at their Housing Office. We work in shifts behind the desk providing support, answering questions, and distributing information about housing alternatives, renting or purchasing, as well as additional materials to help them become better informed. Our purpose is not to pick up prospects. It's all about service, helping those whose work is protecting our country.

G. Dunsten:

You've personally assisted thousands of military families in purchasing and/or selling their homes. What are some of the important characteristics necessary to build a successful career in this niche?

A. Bolin:

Gee, you have to have the heart and mind of service. You must be very flexible and be able to scramble on short notice. The active duty spouse who is going to be deployed, has to know that you will take care of their spouse, as well as the rest of the family here. I tell them, "I'm going to make sure that everything that needs to be done here, will be done. I will take care of it for you." It's a matter of trust. You must show them how sincere you are about their welfare. Often they will come back to Pensacola on multiple tours. It might start out as pilot training, then they return for flight instructor school or they are now commanding a fighter wing or finally, to retire here.

G. Dunsten:

What about referral opportunities?

A. Bolin:

Actually, the military is a close-knit group. Once they find the right person whom they can trust, you become accepted. They will share your name with other military buddies. I am currently working with a number of Navy families in Hawaii that are relocating or will be relocating in the next four months. It's all about building trust and confidence.

Lots of agents act like they care, until the deal is done. After the closing, they scratch them off the list and move on.

G. Dunsten:

What do you do instead?

A. Bolin:

If they were a buyer, I continue to check in on them. I might just pop by 6 weeks after closing and deliver a pie or follow up on how the kids are adjusting in their new school.

Local knowledge is critical. I know their way of life. I understand the challenges and stress the active duty spouse is under and that their primary role is to eliminate any other stress that's not job-related. So I continue to remind them to call me first for anything they need or want to know. I'm always here for them anytime day or night, regardless. You must be their information resource. Remember, they don't know the area. Most of these families are very nervous about hiring people because they often get ripped off.

G. Dunsten:

Why does that happen?

A. Bolin:

It happens because they don't live long enough in one place to know better. In other words, they don't know who is a good, reliable, reasonable, honest painter or repairman. I have an extensive list of service providers that I can count on and refer not only with confidence, but with the understanding that they will take good care of them. I tell all of my allied resources that I expect them to take very good care of our military and bend over backwards for them. I also tell them not to screw up! I never accept any kind of kickback or thank-you gift from a service provider that I refer. Instead, I ask them to give the military client an additional discount off their bill. And they do it!

G. Dunsten:
What do you do about those sellers that are relocating?

A. Bolin:
That's easy! We must remember that our job is to duplicate ourselves, so, at the closing, I tell them that I'm now out of business. I need them to send me someone else like them who is nice to work with. The best place to get the next job is at their closing. I often get a couple of names right on the spot.

G. Dunsten:
I know you and your husband, Mike are very active in your community. What advice do you have for our readers?

A. Bolin:
We all need to give back our time, energy, and financial support as best we can, to our community that benefits us, so find something that you are passionate about and get actively involved.

For us, it's Rotary. We not only help our local chapter, we have helped start additional chapters. We like it because it's international. It allows us to participate in local projects like helping to build a ballpark with rubber turf for handicapped children (called the Miracle Field), to helping raise money for a blood mobile in Costa Rica.

Your success is measured by how much you give back to your community in time and money, showing people that we are more than real estate agents. This is how you can garner more trust and respect.

A. Bolin:
All of the data that is now available doesn't show the buyer or seller enough. People need our guidance and wisdom. We're not selling stock. We're actually the mechanic for real estate. We need to be the person they can go to for advice and we must stay in touch. Also, anything you can do for their kids is a big plus, from a coloring book while touring a home to a toy to play with at closing.

We all have limitations in our area of expertise. I tell my clients, "You are not going to appreciate how much I get paid for what I know and what I do...and you won't appreciate it until something goes wrong and the stuff hits the fan, whether it's about the inspection, financing, paperwork, or negotiating."

Gee, most problems in aviation take place on takeoff or landing. That's where my experience in dealing with these problems comes in.

Remember, our military clients want you to:
1. Take control
2. Put them first
3. Get the job done
4. Continue to build trust
5. Always put their best interests first

If the agent is only concentrating on the money they are going to make, they are not playing in the right game.

Alexis with General Norman Schwarzkopf

Dalton's Take-away:

Alexis has taken the notion of Military Family to heights seldom seen within our Industry. All of us should be doing more to thank America's Heroes. Thank you, Alexis, for what you do.

Chapter 14

Embracing Diversity
an interview with Teresa Palacios Smith
2015 President of The National Association of Hispanic Real Estate Professionals (NAHREP)

by Gee Dunsten

Teresa Smith:

Teresa Palacios Smith is V.P. of Business Development and Cultural Initiatives for Berkshire Hathaway Home Services Georgia Properties. With an extensive background in sales and marketing, Teresa graduated from Mississippi State University, where she received a BA in Broadcasting and Public Relations. The daughter of Hispanic (Colombia, SA) immigrants, Teresa has traveled extensively and is fluent in Spanish. Teresa is a frequent speaker and writer on topics such as Minority Buying, Rental Assistance, Relocation Trends, International Relocation, First Time Home Buying, Successfully Selling HUD Homes and Strategies for Selling Your Home. She has conducted several workshops on these topics and has been published in numerous magazines.

Teresa is ranked as the #1 Latina Real Estate Agent in Georgia and #49 in the country by the National Association of Hispanic Real Estate Professionals (NAHREP) as published in the most recent release of NAHREP's "TOP 250" list. She has been named by the Atlanta Tribune Magazine as one of Atlanta's "Superwomen" for her leadership and advocacy in the Hispanic community. Teresa is the current President-Elect of the National Association of Hispanic Real Estate Professionals (NAHREP) which is one of the largest minority associations in the country with over 20,000 members. Teresa was one of the founding members of the NAHREP Atlanta Chapter which was formed in 2005.

Favorite Quote(s):

"An optimist is a person who sees a green light everywhere, while a pessimist sees only the red stoplight... the truly wise person is colorblind."   – Albert Schweitzer

---

Gee Dunsten:

Teresa, how long have you been in the Real Estate business?

Teresa Smith:

Gee, it's been 20 years. My parents were from Colombia, South America. As a young child, I remember living in a small, two-bedroom apartment in Miami with my parents, grandparents, aunt and uncle. From time to time, my father would remind us that we were living that way so we could buy our own home. Eventually, we did and one home lead to several more homes, propelling our entire family each time to live in a better and better community. The success that we enjoyed (I was the first child in our family to attend and graduate from college) can all be tied back to homeownership and the fact that the number one wealth-creator for the majority of minorities in this country is Real Estate.

G. Dunsten:

So, was that the main reason why you went into Real Estate?

T. Smith:

Yes and no. I've always been very involved with my kids, who are now 23 and 25, as well as, my community, so I selected Real Estate because of its flexible hours. I guess my competitive side, as well as my nature to take on leadership roles, helped me feel comfortable joining the Real Estate ranks. As the result of my Hispanic heritage, and spending most of my formative years growing up in Mississippi, it became important to me to be culturally aware.

G. Dunsten:

Teresa, you are the 2015 President of the National Hispanic Real Estate Professionals and you are currently serving as a rainmaker for Berkshire Hathaway HomeServices Georgia Properties, as well as Vice President for Business Development in Atlanta. What got you on your path to success?

T. Smith:

We all know how important lead generation is to our business. I realized that the relocation side of our business brought lots of people into the Atlanta area from all over the world. So, I persevered to learn everything I could and got involved in the Atlanta Board of Realtors®. Our industry promotes entrepreneurship because most of us are actually business owners. By networking with other successful agents, I became better prepared to run my own successful business within a business. Becoming more proactive in working with Latinos also proved to be a big boost to my business, not to mention that I have always worked across all borders. There was one thing missing, however.

G. Dunsten:

What was that, Teresa?

T. Smith:

The encouragement to get involved on a larger stage with the Hispanic side of the business. It was Dan Foresman, my broker, who invited me to go to Denver to attend a huge Hispanic Real Estate conference. For the first time, I became connected to other top agents across the country, agents that were investing in their communities and focusing on embracing diversity.

G. Dunsten:

What is NAHREP's (National Association of Hispanic Real Estate Professionals) mission?

T. Smith:

Our organization is all about the empowerment of Real Estate. Our goal is to increase sustainable homeownership so that all Latinos can achieve The American Dream. Gee, networking with other minorities should be a greater focus of our industry. Sustainable homeownership is not only good for the immediate family, our neighborhoods, communities, states, and nation, it builds wealth, generates greater pride in where people live, which positively impacts the quality of local education, and has a profound effect on the careers and income of our citizens.

G. Dunsten:
How big is the Hispanic housing population?

T. Smith:
Actually, minority homeownership is quickly becoming the majority in different parts of America. In fact, the Hispanic population is now the majority in eight states, California, Texas, Arizona, and Florida, just to name a few. In fact, the Hispanic population now exceeds 53 million.

G. Dunsten:
How important is homeownership to the Hispanic community?

T. Smith:
Hispanics are passionate about homeownership. It's huge! Family is everything, so homeownership is critical to our quality of life. Everyone strives to fulfill the American Dream of homeownership. It's estimated that by 2020, 50% of homebuyers will be Hispanic. Our current median income is $40,400 and 29% of our population makes between $50,000 and $100,000 per year. One out of every four children born in the U.S. and one out of every three workers in the U.S. is Hispanic, yet our median age is only 27! We have a lot of future homeowners out there.

G. Dunsten:
Teresa, what thoughts and suggestions can you share with our readers about how they can become better equipped to serve this very important segment of the community?

T. Smith:
The key is to take the time to learn and understand our culture and to embrace it. And, you don't have to speak Spanish! Usually, if the parents don't speak English, one of the children does. Anyone can find a friend or relative to play the role of an interpreter.
   1. We're very social.
   2. Family is everything.
   3. Everyone wants to be involved in the process (parents, grandparents, kids, even an aunt, uncle, sister, or brother).
   4. We're passionate about life and the people in it.
   5. We're very loyal, once respect has been established.
   6. We have a natural curiosity about others. So, taking the time to get to know each other and demonstrating transparency, goes a long way. In a sense, you become an

extension of their family.

7. Food, music, and fun are very big. We love to party and enjoy finding reasons to get together with friends to celebrate (which can be a great referral-builder, if you play your cards right).

8. Decision-making can also involve someone like their grandmother, who may not make an appearance or even seem to be involved, only to discover later that her final approval is a must.

9. Getting invited to their home is a huge compliment. Budgeting enough time to not only go, but to have a meaningful visit, can generate big dividends in future business.

10. Taking the time to make a short phone call is always well-received and further enhances the relationship.

G. Dunsten:
What is your best advice when it comes to working with the Hispanic population?

T. Smith:
Gee, Wayne Gretzky said, "You miss 100% of the shots you never take." So, don't be afraid to get into the game and to take the shot. Get involved. Learn more about our culture. Look up organizations in your area to participate in.

Our industry is behind the curve. We need to recruit more agents to better serve our different cultures and expand our horizons, as well as, create an atmosphere of curiosity and enlightenment, so we all can become better ambassadors for our communities, and, at the same time, provide more relevant content and service to all types of customers and clients.

Dalton's Take-away:

Wayne Gretzky, who interestingly lives in my town of Westlake Village, California (although I'm sure he is not aware I live in town), also is credited with saying, "The key to my success was not in skating to the puck but, instead, skating to where the puck was going to be." Teresa is elegantly and passionately alerting our Industry that not only is the Hispanic population a major contributor to both the Real Estate economy, as well as the greater American economy, but with a median age of only 27, that this remarkably impressive segment of Americans will continue to grow, succeed, and (along with Teresa and her leadership) skate out in front.

I was also impressed with how Teresa credits her Nationally respected Broker, Dan Foresman, with inspiring her to pursue this particular segment of the market. It suggests to me that every Broker and manager in the country should become fully versed with all the National Association of Realtors® offers in terms of organizations that can help enhance the niche marketing efforts of their Realtor® Associates.

Chapter 15

Creating Connections Through Local Community Organizations
an interview with Leon Lopes
Exclusive TownAdvisor Member for Plymouth, MA

by Gee Dunsten

Leon Lopes:

Leon of Re/Max SPECTRUM has been a Licensed Real Estate Sales Professional in Massachusetts since 1994, specializing in helping Sellers and Buyers in the sale, marketing, or purchase of a home in the Plymouth, MA area. His concentration is on residential property, including Single Family, Condominium, Waterfront, New Construction and The Pinehills. In addition, he's been involved with Land and Commercial real estate transactions. Leon is a member of the National Association of Realtors®, Massachusetts Association of Realtors® and Plymouth and South Shore Association of Realtors®. He is also a member of the Institute for Luxury Home Marketing and has achieved the Certified Luxury Home Marketing Specialist and E-Pro designations. Leon is a member of the RE/MAX Hall of Fame, RE/MAX Platinum Club and RE/MAX 100% Club. Leon is a life-long resident of the South Shore and has enjoyed being involved with numerous local organizations including the Rotary Club of Plymouth, Plymouth Area Community Television (PACTV), Plymouth Area Chamber of Commerce, Pilgrim Hall Museum, Old Colony YMCA, and local town government. His number one goal is a truly satisfied client who is confident in referring Leon to anyone needing the services of a professional Realtor®.

Favorite Quote:

"Character may be manifested in the great moments, but it is made in the small ones."
– Winston Churchill

Gee Dunsten:

When did you get into the real estate business, Leon?

Leon Lopes:

Actually, I started working part-time in 1994, while I was also working in a management position with a regional retail discount department chain and was traveling back and forth to their corporate headquarters. I was not sure I would actually like it, but I finally decided to quit my management job and go full-time in 1997.

G. Dunsten:

What helped you make a smooth transition from part-time to a successful full-time agent in Plymouth, MA?

L. Lopes:

Gee, it was a couple of things. My retail management background taught me the importance of providing great customer service, as well as the importance of developing a team environment between departments/participants in the transaction. Based on my organizational skills, strong connection to our local community, and encouragement from my manager and mentor, I decided to focus on homeowners.

G. Dunsten:
What are some of your keys to success?

L. Lopes:
That's a good question, Gee. Actually, I have to admit I'm a control freak. The process of managing every listing became an obsession, so I developed the Lopes Team, which consists of a buyer's agent, great mortgage rep, title person, home inspector, stager, etc. We continue to strive for perfection from the time the home goes on the market, to how we market, negotiate, and handle all the details from contract, all the way to closing.

Also, over the last 30 years, I have made it a high priority to establish connections and build relationships through my involvement in some of the clubs and organizations in our Plymouth community, and as a result, many of these connections/friendships have had a big impact on the success of my business.

G. Dunsten:
How important has your community involvement been to your great success?

L. Lopes:
Oh, it's had an enormous impact. To be a real professional you must be connected with other professionals and most of the top professionals, the movers and shakers, are active participants in our local clubs, organizations, and community resources. The Chamber of Commerce is huge. It's the epicenter of our business community. There are always a number of active committees and projects to support. Rolling your sleeves up to volunteer and doing the best job you can on any task or assignment you take on, will build credibility and top-of-the-mind awareness with a cross-section of members.

Because Plymouth is a destination, from April to November it is often overrun with out-of-town visitors, and the small staff at the Chamber can always use an extra hand. They frequently look for partnerships within the business community.

G. Dunsten:
Leon, how do you go about leveraging relationships?

L. Lopes:
Well, Gee in addition to maintaining contact with past clients, for a number of years now I've participated in our Chamber's Ambassador Program, which involves attending monthly networking sessions. It's a great way to learn more about what's going on in town, as well as a great way to build relationships with other business leaders at the same time. It's a time commitment, but the rewards are many. The Chamber also

sponsors Business-After-Hours and Morning Mixers on a monthly basis. I make it a huge priority and try to attend as many as possible with the intention of getting to introduce at least two people and/or have at least two people introduce me to two other people I don't already know.

G. Dunsten:

Are there any other clubs or organizations you can recommend?

L. Lopes:

Rotary Club is also a great organization, because they do a lot to support a number of charities and non-profit service organizations. I've been a member of our local club for fifteen years. Our annual auction is a huge event that is held on TV and broadcast to six local towns. Helping to solicit donations not only gives you a great deal of satisfaction, at the same time it allows you to get to know many of your neighbors. In a way, most of our real estate business is a by-product of our community involvement. While serving for six years as an elected town meeting representative, I got a wonderful, hands-on education in our local government, its structure and participants, as well as, who to see or where to go for assistance with the different types of challenges my clients might be faced with, such as zoning issues or permit problems. In fact, many of my friends call me "Sponge." The more you learn about your community, the more credible you become, especially when relocation opportunities present themselves.

G. Dunsten:

Do you have any closing thoughts or recommendations you'd like to share, Leon?

L. Lopes:

Pick something that you are passionate about and get involved. Take it slow. You can't get so distracted that it takes away from servicing your primary clients. Remember, it's not about prospecting or networking, it's about reinforcing your brand and commitment to your community. Garner a reputation for getting things done!

And, lastly, there is no better way to connect with local town businesses and residents than to be seen as fully committed to protect and enhance local home values. This is why I became the exclusive Member for TownAdvisor with a town website about how great it is to live there and tell everyone about it; which I do.

144

Leon and Plymouth's treasured National Monument to the Forefathers and Mayflower 2.

Dalton's Take-away:

Leon represents the perfect example of when a Realtor® lives within a town, where the town itself can generate a significant number of listings, it is worthwhile (beyond pure civic motivations) to invest strategic time with town or city organizations.

Plymouth's population is in excess of 50,000 and the average sales price is approaching $400,000. This means that the Plymouth community of homeowners, in its own right, can generate attractive ROI.

When you live in a town of 5 to 10 thousand people, and where the average price is materially less, greater emphasis might be warranted toward the regional communities of FSBOs, Expireds, general Homeowners, etc. as this might represent a better ROI than making major commitments to the civic enterprises of any one town or city.

Although Leon, like most Realtors®, does business in multiple communities, it's impressive how special he makes homeowners uniquely feel within Plymouth, his major source of business.

And, like all other chapter contributors, Leon's overall business plan is being limited to just one subject, community organizations. This is the reason why this is one of our briefest chapters and speaks to only a very minor part of all that Leon does to be successful.

Chapter 16

Seasonal Communities/Second Homes
an interview with Linda Rike
Exclusive TownAdvisor Member for Morehead City, NC

by Gee Dunsten

Linda Rike:

Linda was born in Washington, North Carolina and moved to Carteret County in 1965. She earned a master's degree in education with an emphasis in counseling from East Carolina University and then returned to the Crystal Coast of North Carolina to embark on her Real Estate career: Linda Rike Realty.

"I love where I grew up and wanted to help other people discover the charming lifestyle that is so predominant here. Working in Real Estate allows me to be instrumental in introducing others to the amenities and beauty of all Carteret County - Beaufort, Morehead City, Pine Knoll Shores and Atlantic Beach."

Favorite Quote:

"The Road to Happiness lies in two simple principles: find what it is that interests you and that you can do well, and when you find it put your whole soul into it - every bit of energy and ambition and natural ability you have." – John D Rockefeller III

Gee Dunsten:
When did you get into Real Estate?

Linda Rike:
I started in 1985. I realized that I was making more money buying and selling properties than teaching Special Ed with a Master's Degree. After using the same agent, who wasn't dependable or very professional, I decided I could do a better job than they could.

G. Dunsten:
What percentage of your business comes from vacation/second home buyers?

L. Rike:
60% are vacation or investor home buyers and 40% are year-round homeowners.

G. Dunsten:
How different is working with vacation/second home buyers/sellers versus primary homeowners/buyers?

L. Rike:
We never meet many of our second homeowners face-to-face. We have lots of communication, usually by phone and/or email. The sale is all about trust. It's building and getting their confidence in our ability to get their home sold or find them a great investment.

G. Dunsten:

How do you do it?

L. Rike:

It starts with building awareness about our market and community knowledge, as well as getting results. We have been doing a lot of direct mail for over 20 years, from "Just Sold" and "Just Listed" postcards, to calendars.

G. Dunsten:

That's a lot of postage, isn't it?

L. Rike:

We actually spend between $2,000 and $3,000 a month on postage and we've been doing that for years.

G. Dunsten:

How do you stay organized?

L. Rike:

We have over 40,000 people's names, addresses, and phone numbers in our database. It's actually divided into subsets or sections:

1. Special waterfront properties
2. Condominium complexes
3. Community where I live
4. Beachfront
5. Primary residences
6. Vacant lots, etc.

Gee, we continue to update and add new names to our database on a weekly basis and actually pay someone to provide us with a count report every week, listing everything that has sold and/or transferred.

G. Dunsten:

What kind of information do they provide?

L. Rike:

It's broken down by property type:

1. Vacant lots
2. Condominiums
3. Single-family
4. Waterfront, etc.

It also includes the seller's information, as well as, the purchaser's, including their permanent address.

G. Dunsten:
What do you do with all of this data?

L. Rike:
In many situations, we add them to our database and, depending upon where the property is located, they are placed in one of our 'drip campaigns'. I've had situations where we started to drip them with postcards, in the same way that we treat our past customers and, years later, they came back to us to buy, sell, or refer a friend, even though we weren't involved in either side of their original transaction. I like to refer to them as some of our adopted clients who were orphaned by their agents.

G. Dunsten:
You mentioned drip campaigns. How often do you contact your clients?

L. Rike:
Gee, that depends upon our relationship. Almost everyone hears from us at least four times a year with a postcard. If something happens in their area, like a sale or a new listing, we send them a postcard. Our postcards are designed to generate new listings. We use different postcards for different situations and/or targets. Our primary goal is to remind everyone that we are listing and selling properties every week. We also let them know about activities and events that are happening in our area. When the market is running strong, we increase our number of contacts. Our local past clients and current customers get a supply of seasonal return address labels, however, to get them, they must stop by our office (face-to-face). Our new listings and price reductions postcards go out weekly, targeted to homeowners in those neighborhoods or to out-of-town buyer prospects.

G. Dunsten:
Who does your postcards?

L. Rike:
We have a local printer that produces color postcard shells on one side and our contact and postal information in black on the other side. They come 4 up. When we get a new listing, we print the information ourselves on the back side of the postcard. In the course of a year, we go through a lot of ink!

G. Dunsten:

You mentioned calendars. Tell us about them.

L. Rike:

We mail out a refrigerator magnetic calendar to over 1,000 of our best out-of-town clients with first-class postage. In fact, Gee, everything we mail out is first-class postage. It's very important to maintain a first-class image in everything you do. We also distribute over two hundred and fifty 8½" x 11"calendars. Because of the cost and popularity, we send out a postcard in mid-September asking them to call us to reserve their calendar. (This is another way to get to talk to them directly). If they are local, we call them when the calendars arrive to invite them to stop by our office to pick theirs up. Those brief, face-to-face visits at our office, generate leads that turn into transactions every year.

G. Dunsten:

What do you mail out to any buyer or seller inquiries?

L. Rike:

As you know, Gee, today's prospects have almost always been online doing research about what's for sale, as well as, our area, so we always ask, "Do you have a large area map?" 99.9% say, "Actually, we don't." My response is always, "Let me send you a BIG, very detailed area map to help you locate property locations, restaurants, beaches, and more." They love it and it instantly starts to create trust and more conversation.

G. Dunsten:

Linda, how important is your community involvement?

L. Rike:

I think most agents are actually small business owners. As a business owner, we have a responsibility to help our community grow and prosper. Everyone should pick several interests that they feel warm and fuzzy about and where they can make a difference by donating some of their time and/or money.

About 15 years ago, we became the only sponsor for our Big Rock Blue Marlin International Tournament, because it brings a lot of money into our community, while, at the same time, raises millions of dollars for our local charities. It's a week-long event that brings the entire community together for this wonderful cause. We have a booth, help sell raffle tickets, participate in the printing and distribution of over 26,000 tee shirts, and much more. Recently, we've taken an active leadership role in the revitalization of downtown Morehead City. Most Realtors® are joiners, but what your community needs is people helping in leadership roles. In today's market, the consumer wants a local advisor, not

150

just a tour guide. The more active you are, the more you'll learn and know. Most agents

don't realize that most out-of-town buyers are considering different community options. We compete against other beaches in North Carolina, South Carolina, and Virginia. The response to our Town Advisor Real Estate Town Docu-Mentary^{SM} has been terrific. When you offer to send them a mini movie that you've created about your town, they are overwhelmed.

Also, we always take buyers on a car tour of our main roads and side roads, so we can teach them things about our community – from its history to the best fishing hole, to the safest beach; things that you have to be a local to know. We're telling a story. That's why our motto is, "Just Add Water to Your Lifestyle!"

G. Dunsten:

What's your best advice to our readers?

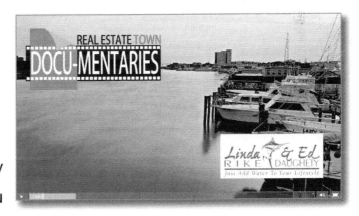

L. Rike:

Become a student of your community and your local Real Estate market. You must know everything or where to find it. Find out what they like. Determine what their primary reasons are for buying. Are they an investor, vacation home, or future year-round resident? Everyone wants to know that they made a good investment.

G. Dunsten:

So Linda, what's your definition of a good investment?

L. Rike:

You know it's a good investment if:

1. You can sleep at night

2. You can ride by and look at it once in a while

3. You don't have to feed it much

4. You get use and enjoyment out of it - It's those photos of family and friends – the memories are priceless.

Dalton's Take-away:

Linda officially has a Masters Degree in Education yet, unofficially, has a "Ph.D." in Community Marketing. All one has to do is emulate just some of the many concrete specifics she provides here in the book, and you too, like her investors, will sleep better at night.

Chapter 17

<u>"Helping Communities Storm Back"</u>
<u>after Natural Disasters</u>
an interview with Larry Vecchio

*Founder and broker of Better Homes Realty offices throughout Coastal & Central New Jersey
& Co-founder of Town Advisor.com*

by Allan Dalton

Lawrence Vecchio:

Lawrence Vecchio has served as Broker Owner of Better Homes Realty since January 1980. "Larry" oversees 300 Sales Associates who work throughout the U.S. Vecchio is also founder and president of VRI Realty, Inc. Better Homes Realty and Condo Domain, based in Hazlet, NJ.

Co-founder of Townadvisor.com and the Real Estate Town Advisors[SM] Network, Vecchio is a frequent speaker at real estate conferences and a consultant on web-based real estate initiatives.

<u>Favorite Quote:</u>

"A ship in harbor is safe, but that is not what ships are built for." – John A. Shedd

---

Allan Dalton:

Larry, before we discuss the prominent and positive role that you and your company played in the aftermath of the Sandy storm, I must say that walking through the various towns in your market (and seeing how local residents respond to you) leaves me wondering, "Why haven't you run for Governor?" How do you account for this immense level of community connectivity?

Larry Vecchio:

It begins with my family. My father, may he rest in peace, was a musician with the fabled Viscounts. While their band enjoyed some degree of national prominence and appeared on American Bandstand, they were legendary throughout our New Jersey communities, where The Four Seasons (known at the time as The Four Lovers) would open for them.

Seeing how my Dad and his group created such happiness through their music, meant that I too wanted to please others. But, since I won't even sing in the shower, I needed to find other means.

A. Dalton:

Gee, you would think that The Viscounts would have been mentioned in the Jersey Boys play and movie. What jealously!

L. Vecchio:

But seriously, Allan, there is a true connection between family and community. My wife, Patty, has always been active in our church and community charities. My son, Larry, works with legendary homebuilder Hovnanian, who actually builds housing communities. Our

154

daughters, Nina and Lauren, are both school teachers in our local communities, and my three brothers' community involvement ranges from fireman to insurance and mortgage brokerages. Therefore, we are a "full service" community family.

My son Larry will build your home. My brother Mark will finance it. My brother Joe will insure it. I will sell it and my daughters' will teach your children in our schools.

A. Dalton:
And if I am right Larry, in addition to your Dad's iconic musical status in New Jersey's local communities, he also cut hair as the local barber.

L. Vecchio:
Yes. Starting with my wife and I who were high school sweethearts, we are "all in" when it comes to our communities.

A. Dalton:
Larry, how did this lifetime of community involvement, and all the connections you made, help you to first grow your Real Estate business... and then impact your community leadership role regarding The Sandy Recovery efforts?

L. Vecchio:
Well, Allan, building our company throughout all of our communities has been a natural outgrowth and evolution of being from a family of community activists... and, as the saying goes, "I hired in my own image." I looked for managers, who then looked for associates, who were of and for their communities.

A. Dalton:
Now, before we specifically discuss Sandy I must get something out of the way. Larry in my entire life I have never seen anyone who walks through life with a perpetual smile as you do. How is this greeted within your communities?

L. Vecchio:
It's funny you say that, as basically, I have been told the same thing ever since I was a child... and I think I got it from my Dad.
In fact, when I was in high school, I used to walk by a grocery store where, occasionally, the owner would stand outside with a few of his friends. One day, as I approached, he announced to his buddies, "Look who's coming... Smiley!"

A. Dalton:
Larry, let's move on to how you helped New Jersey "storm back." What were your objectives in providing leadership and how did you accomplish them?

L. Vecchio:

Well, when Sandy hit us, it was one of the few times in my life that I lost my smile. In fact, as I drove around with one of my associates touring the biblical-like damage of the storm that ranked as the second costliest hurricane in U.S. history (and the worst hurricane the Atlantic coast has experienced in recorded history), my associate must have seen a tear drop from my eye as he said, "Larry, you remind me of that old commercial where 'Chief' Iron Eyes Cody is shown with a tear dropping from his eye as he looks out over the pollution of his environment."

A. Dalton:

Boy, that's vivid. Take me through your steps from the outset of this epic storm.

L. Vecchio:

First, as our home was severely damaged, it meant moving my family to a rental. Step two was calling all of our managers, and making a list, so that all our associates and their families would be contacted by the company to see what emergency measures were necessary for them and their families. After that, it was all about our larger communities' needs.

A. Dalton:

And what did your plan and activities consist of?

L. Vecchio:

I know it sounds a little corny to say that I created a five point plan, but I actually did. I planned to:

1. Make our offices available as shelters, providing blankets and food for our newly created homeless

2. Find a way to help the community protect their properties

3. Provide assistance through the collaborative efforts with federal, state, and local government agencies, as well as legal and insurance assistance

4. Protect our residents from out-of-state profiteers who looked at our communities as profit opportunities versus local vendors looking to help fellow citizens to rebuild

5. Create a campaign and websites to educate our communities and announce our numerous community relief seminars. I had previously created BetterHomesforAll.com – along with how our company mission statement included a commitment to helping the

156

homeless. I am additionally grateful that my Better Homes family also rallied behind how BetterHomesforAll.com and also sponsored an event for homeless animals. In the aftermath of Sandy, I knew I needed to create a completely distinct campaign to exclusively aid storm victims.

A. Dalton:

Larry, before we discuss your Sandy-related campaign, let me inform our readers that you purchased a condo and donated it to a local women's shelter. But now, in terms of the campaign, tell me about it.

L. Vecchio:

As I toured our communities and met with all those who sought relief and food at our offices, I was struck by the collective dismay that was so evident. As a result, I came up with the idea of introducing (through banners, websites, and t-shirts, etc.) the following slogan: "Storming back for Shore."

I felt that the play on words (shore versus sure and "storming back") would provide the optimism that our communities were desperately looking for, and would suggest that we were using the word "storm" (a word that was on the minds of our citizens, perhaps more than any other word in their lifetime) as a word that we could now turn around and together, "storm back" to rebuild with the same level of fury... as was evidenced by the negative force from this natural disaster.

A. Dalton:

Larry, when I saw these t-shirts and banners I thought, "How ironic!," as I still had the image in my mind (from the New Orleans National Association of Realtors® Convention) of you actually buying a house in full, for a Katrina victim... and now, here you go again (as some after-storm superhero), helping your own communities.

L. Vecchio:

Allan, I'm no superhero. When my wife and I discussed Katrina, it was Patty who said, "Larry, we need to do something... that could be our home!" Ironically, later, it was not only our home but some of my offices as well that were destroyed.

A. Dalton:

How did you use your unscathed offices as part of the relief effort?

L. Vecchio:

My corporate headquarters was actually kidded about (by FEMA officials, The Red Cross, and the folks from Sandy New Jersey Relief Fund), as being the "unofficial storm relief headquarters" for The Shore.

Not only did I put together teams of federal, state and local officials (lawyers, mold inspectors, engineers, geologists, insurance companies, etc.), all who met at my offices regularly to form our series of community Sandy Relief Seminars (which were held at hotels, restaurants, and our own local offices), I also used

Vecchio leading Relief Team efforts.

our office as the venue to launch a company wide reach-out and education program. These agencies appreciated that I asked all of our associates to "put their boots on" and (in some cases, grab row boats) and go door-to-door handing out pamphlets and flyers that offered advice on how to reach out for help.

Larry Vecchio personally donating a home to a Katrina victim.

A. Dalton:

Clearly, someone who donates a fully paid home for a Katrina victim from their own personal family funds, does not reach out for personal or company gain. Did the old adage "that by giving, we receive" lead to your company doing more business?

L. Vecchio:

Absolutely. My associates found that my insistence that they go door-to-door, inadvertently became, as Gee Dunsten likes to call it, "completely, rejection-free prospecting!"

The benefits to our company have been huge. People in our towns immediately grasp who authentically cares, and my people do care, and I care about them, because they care about their communities.

A. Dalton:

Larry, lastly, let me ask you how this experience contributed to your being a co-founder (along with myself) of TownAdvisor.com?

L. Vecchio:

There's a powerful connection here between my involvement with the Sandy recovery efforts and TownAdvisor.com

Sandy taught me how deeply town residents care about not only their family and home, but their town at large.

The people in Lavallette (where we have a vacation home at the shore, and where I am on the homeowners association board) were more concerned with what happened to Lavallette than what happened to Rumson. Rumson homeowners viewed Sandy more in terms of what it did to Rumson than Spring Lake, etc. We saw this through our events. Local residents looked for direction from their local town officials along with the state and federal agencies.

TownAdvisor.com celebrates Americas's towns and cities as individual entities; each with its own story, history, and distinct community appeal... all of which needs to be wonderfully conveyed online and through town videos.

Another way Larry Vecchio and company associates, Debbie Klein & Michelle Irizarry, support their community.

A. Dalton:

Larry, thank you for all you do for your fellow citizens, and thus, your Industry.

Dalton's Take-away:

Apologies to Larry for having his story told in this book instead of sending it to the CNN Heroes Program.

Larry has developed and runs multiple community-based businesses throughout New Jersey, all of which are extensions of his family's legacy of always putting the community first.

Chapter 18

Unlocking Gated and Golf Communities
an interview with Jack O'Connor
Exclusive TownAdvisor Member for Castle Rock, CO

by Gee Dunsten

Jack O'Connor:

Jack O'Connor started his Real Estate career in 1979 and became a top producer in a 700 sales agent firm. He has participated in over 2500+ transactions and has sold in excess of $410 million in sales volume. Jack is the Broker Owner for The Denver 100, LLC, an innovative Real Estate services company in the Denver Metro area. Jack has been recognized as "Manager of the Year" by a large Denver firm and was awarded the "Executive of the Year" for innovative leadership techniques, in addition to being nominated as Ernst and Young's Entrepreneur of the Year. During Jack's career he has been considered a creative Real Estate mind, innovator of brokerage programs others have duplicated and personally has trained and coached over 1500 brokers nationwide. He has spoken nationally and internationally on management and sales topics.

Favorite Quote:

"I tell you the truth, whoever hears my word and believes him who sent me has eternal life and will not be condemned, he has crossed over from death to life." – John 5:24

Gee Dunsten:

Jack, why did you enter Real Estate as a profession?

Jack O'Connor:

I entered Real Estate as a professional athlete who had given lessons to some Real Estate brokers of the time. I felt I could compete with the competition in this field. So far, 34 years later, it's worked. For the past 15 years, my greatest emphasis has been to develop luxury homes and golf course communities around suburban Denver.

G. Dunsten:

What led you to develop a special focus on the vacation home particular market or segment of the community?

J. O'Connor:

I have focused on Luxury Homes in Golf Communities around Denver. I enjoy golf and can play a decent round of golf. By having people that want to play golf with me, and my knowledge of the golf community markets, many doors have opened to obtaining business all over the Denver community. I've also traveled extensively to play golf around the world, so the stories I bring back make me somewhat of a celebrity amateur golfer in their eyes. I am far from being that good, but golf is a game that you can play with virtually any level of golfer, as you both play against the course, not the individual. Being a golf storyteller and knowing each and every golf community I play within, exhibits an expertise that intrigues people to learn more, and not just about golf, but about Real Estate and the trends within the community.

161

G. Dunsten:

What differentiates your approach vs. others in serving this market?

J. O'Connor:

I would say I know more about the trends within each community than most Real Estate brokers. I study and take an in-depth approach to knowing the supply and demand of each luxury market and the floor plan/designs that are hot for today's marketplace. In many luxury homes, homeowners have built specific homes that met their needs at the time, with little regard for general buyer behaviors when they end up selling. We have a full team of "Jack O'Connor's Enhanced Service Package," which includes, stagers, architects, handymen, cleaning crews, moving concierge, appraisers, measurement services, pre-inspection programs and a complete online market presence unique to my listings. I utilize some, if not all, these groups on each listing and since I am including these costs within my fees, it becomes a very attractive package for the luxury homeowner, who typically, just wants to get the home sold without having to manage the obsolescence of the property. From a historical and productive standpoint, offering a full-service, luxury commission package, will clearly unlock their gate.

G. Dunsten:

What are some specific things you are doing that contribute to your remarkable success?

J. O'Connor:

I have created a pre-marketing system called "The Denver 100 Ten-Day Listing Launch." The basics of this program are designed to create an online presence for those tens of thousands of online lookers and to move them to buyers before the home hits the market. We are selling 18% of our own listings with this program over the first 30 days of the listing period. I would also suggest the use of our "Enhanced Services Package," which has been a huge point of difference for me in my market. By the way, learning to package my programs resulted from a 1983 national conference in Boston, where Allan was the keynote speaker for the Better Homes and Gardens franchisees. The topic was "The Better Homes and Gardens Home marketing System." Not a listing presentation, but a package of services that moves with each market. An ingenious idea that I still use as my basis for selling Real Estate today.

G. Dunsten:

Why is this an important market?

J. O'Connor:

This is the first market I have witnessed in 30+ years that has allowed a mid-priced property to appreciate at 8% per year for the last 3 years and afford that homeowner the

162

opportunity to move up to a luxury home in a community for their family. With interest rates at historically low levels and luxury home prices in Denver still adjusting downward, a homeowner has the greatest single window of opportunity to get into a neighborhood/ community at the most attractive financial time. I write a blog that highlights this phenomenon each month. We title the Blog, "So How's the Market." An idea Allan gave me in 1992. It has worked all this time in capturing the attention of home buyers and sellers.

G. Dunsten:
What percentage of your time do you devote to efforts surrounding these community-based services (or marketing efforts)?

J. O'Connor:
I am involved with quite a bit of the social and charitable aspects of the golf communities, whether it's playing in the local golf tournament or hosting golf outings for others to come visit the community and course. I would estimate that more than 50% of my relationship-building time is within the communities that I serve."

G. Dunsten:
Jack, I love your term, relationship-building time. Why do you believe others have not done what you're doing?

J. O'Connor:
It costs money to join golf clubs and to play golf. It also costs money to have social functions at golf outings. I treat these expenditures as any other business would in building their business. There is little to write off on taxes, but what other job in the world could I have that I get to play great golf courses, with really interesting people who happen to live in one million dollar homes? America is a great place to play and work. Effectively, assimilating these elite communities also requires a healthy self-image, not only to become accepted in their community, but to be perceived as a leader when it comes to their Real Estate needs and requests.

G. Dunsten:
How do you define your geographical market?

J. O'Connor:
When I first started out in my career, my geographical area was everybody in every place. While making a transition from being an athlete to a business person, I was literally, all over the map. Over time, my level of strategic approach dramatically evolved into 3 specific categories:

163

1. Target-niche marketing of gated golf communities

2. Strengthening our referral satisfaction

3. Luxury home clients outside of the gates

G. Dunsten:
How did you determine which segments of the community you decided to "marketize"?

J. O'Connor:
It was easy to find golf communities with gates. I just needed to get inside them.

G. Dunsten:
I didn't hear any mention of buyers, Jack.

J. O'Connor:
I am very selective as to which buyer I will serve, which means I will always work with buyer referrals from important clients and high conversion rate transferees. Other than that, I look to delegate all other buyers to an associate who can devote the necessary time to provide the level of service that all buyers deserve.

G. Dunsten:
What percentage of your business is from home sellers versus home buyers?

J. O'Connor:
80% home sellers, 20% home buyers, however, I have noticed that a large segment of buyers in the last three years have come from our pre-marketing of my listings in golf communities. Many buyers today find my listings before they find a buyer's agent. Having a strong listing inventory has never been more important.

G. Dunsten:
How do you integrate your offline and online marketing and networking efforts?

J. O'Connor:
I am a baby boomer, so most of my leads are generated offline via contacts with current clients. That is my largest source of lead generation. I have a social media presence, but my marketing coordinator really includes personal and business in a balanced message online, which I believe, keeps my name in front of thousands of people 3 to 4 times per month. I do both snail mail and e-mail marketing 36 times per year to my target group of 300 people.

164

G. Dunsten:
I love the two things you just said, Jack.
1. You recognize the disproportion of value of offline engagements.
2. You have an effective system.

What percentage of your business comes from offline marketing?

J. O'Connor:
90% of my business comes from offline lead generation. Being face-to-face with people in comfortable situations allows them to refer me more business.

G. Dunsten:
Have you ever prospected door-to-door? If so, what was your approach and how frequently did you do this?

J. O'Connor:
I did door-to-door early in my career with huge success, however, I got burned out within 4 years of prospecting door-to-door. Most luxury markets in Denver would have a difficult time with door-to-door solicitation, however I am excited about my new plan to go door-to-door distributing my Real Estate-Town Docu-Mentary[SM] DVD, created for me by Town Advisor, except in those communities where it isn't permissible.

G. Dunsten:
Are you more of a prospector, networker, offline marketer, or online social networker (and I am sure you do them all)?

J. O'Connor:
I am most certainly a networker and obtain business from my network's connections.

G. Dunsten:
What have you done to build your personal brand in your community?

J. O'Connor:
The Denver 100 was a brand new company in 2011. It is now recognized as a leader in Real Estate in just under 4 years. We have done that with our success. We are selling 35 homes per month with an average price of $475,000, which is $150K over the Denver home average.

G. Dunsten:
How much of your business is from open houses?

J. O'Connor:

We do about 12 open houses per week, as that is part of our "Listing Launch" system. We believe open houses are the way to attract online buyers faster than any other method we could create, as they are looking to get into a home. We do open houses on Thursday, Friday, and Saturday afternoons as part of our "Sneak Peek Neighborhood" preview systems.

G. Dunsten:

How much longer do you plan to continue working in Real Estate in such a fully committed way?

J. O'Connor:

I am enjoying my work and have a passion to get up and go to work each day. I cannot fathom not selling Real Estate over the next 20 years and would like to look at expanding our company over that period to a maximum of 100 brokers, averaging 20 transactions per year. I am not under the belief that the future of Real Estate brokerage is having more agents. I believe having a commando unit of top producers with neighborhood and community involvement are the conduits to selling Real Estate in the next decade.

G. Dunsten:

What is your advice to the Real Estate industry as a whole for necessary change?

J. O'Connor:

Become more professional. We have allowed third parties to take over the position of being the knowledge source of Real Estate. No online experience can equal what we can provide in trends and knowledge of the market, so get more professionals who know the market and know the trends in valuation of properties.

G. Dunsten:

How much importance do you place on continuing to learn, as it relates to your success?

J. O'Connor:

Old dogs must learn new tricks to stay competitive, whether it's a tool to use, such as a smartphone or tablet, or a new law that will affect the trends in Real Estate. Staying updated and current is critical to competing. As I say to my friends, I may be slower, but I am smarter in how I approach the game. I like the saying, "When one is through changing, one is through," as it also applies to the importance of education. Any Realtor® who believes education represents their past, has no future in our business.

G. Dunsten:

What is the one thing that you do to create Real Estate connections that you wish you had started earlier?

166

J. O'Connor:

Oh my. I made every mistake possible in prospecting during the first five years in real estate. Although I sold a lot of homes, I did it through sheer "A-type" personality skills, not Real Estate skills. I didn't understand the value of networking and the value of knowing the marketplace better than the competition. Had I started with market knowledge first, then networking second, I would be so far ahead. When coaching a brand new licensee in today's world, part of their job description in working with me is to be inside 5 homes per day, every day of their first year. You cannot imagine how that shortens the learning curve in obtaining business. I also wish I had learned earlier how important it is to demonstrate to the entire community that we are promoting the whole value of the community.

G. Dunsten:

If you had a son or daughter (and if you do, answer it from that perspective) entering the business, what would be the top three things you would tell them they must do if they are to be successful?

J. O'Connor:

I would tell him/her to…

1. Get inside homes every day
2. Have a compelling story of your "why" for selling Real Estate
3. Learn to network with a target group that parallels the passions/hobbies you like to do and that you are comfortable talking to people about

G. Dunsten:

In what parts of your business do you have either administrative help or team support?

J. O'Connor:

I like to manage my own transactions, because of the exclusivity of the clients I represent. This group also is my biggest referral source, so I do not delegate this part, which I see a lot of brokers do. I delegate all open houses, the online leads and lead generation system, and all marketing online and in print. Everything else I do, as I will sell about 25 homes per year at an average price of $750,000, so it's manageable. If my average price was substantially less, I would delegate a lot more of the transaction systems.

G. Dunsten:

How do you deal with jealousy among colleagues (if applicable), regarding your success?

J. O'Connor:

I don't make a big deal about my sales volume. I let my actions speak for my success and others follow that and like to pick my brain. I meet once a week with my sales team to go over dialogues for that week, new trends and to make sure we are all moving in the same direction. I haven't had an agent leave in 14 months, except for one I fired for misconduct.

G. Dunsten:
How would you rate our industry in general, regarding being community- and consumer-centric vs. self-centered in how we engage our overall community in general?

J. O'Connor:
The Real Estate industry is moving from a service industry to a transaction industry. What I mean by that is the new model of Real Estate brokerage is to have as many agents as possible and hope they sell something, regardless of the service they pro-vide. I believe this is driving even more consumers away from true profession-als in Real Estate. We describe our job as a "lobbyist" and perform at the high-est level to meet the client's goals, not a "hobbyist," who may sell 4 homes per year with no concern over a long-term business relationship with the client or how the transaction will make them feel. The better the marketplace has been in number of sales, has yet to expose the "hobbyist" in its pure intent, but it's in-evitable. If the transaction doesn't feel special to the consumer, they will find another pathway to take. I would like to think that by my engagement in helping

"Making connections by combining my vocation and advocation."

maintain laws friendly to homeownership, helping maintain innovative marketing to bring buyers who buy the home at the highest realistic price, building communi-ties where families enjoy living, and creating systems that make the transaction smoother for all parties, encourages future clients to choose this pathway to take.

Dalton's Take-away:
To me, it requires a very evolved individual to skillfully combine one's avocation and vocation. Jack is a great golfer because he is a student of the game, and an even greater Realtor® because he has acquired a "Phd" in Real Estate Marketing. Congratulations, Jack!

Chapter 19

<u>The Don'ts and Do's of Creating Customized Community Videos</u>

an interview by Allan Dalton with a practitioner panel consisting of:
Julie Vanderblue, Gee Dunsten, Jack O'Connor and Pam Charron

Allan Dalton:

The Real Estate Industry has long fought against the perception held by many consumers, that all Real Estate Professionals are essentially similar in terms of the skills they possess and the services they provide.

Did the desire to further differentiate yourself influence your decision to produce a community video?

Julie Vanderblue:

Well, considering how all industry professionals have equal access to IDX, MLS, Realtor.com, Trulia and Zillow... along with many shared activities and resources, like Open Houses and For Sale signs, etc.... the need to display a level of differentiation that immediately registers with consumers, and especially with homeowners, was a major factor in my producing town videos for the nine towns I principally serve in Fairfield County. Everyone in our business markets "homes," therefore, in order to truly differentiate oneself requires also specializing in a different category or subset of overall marketing. Specifically, since, as yet, most Realtors® do not market "towns and cities" with the same level of "marketing muscle" behind their efforts as when they market individual properties, differentiation relating to "town or city promotion" is an amazingly easy and effective way to completely differentiate yourself to prospective homeseller clients.

Thus, the rewards generated (in terms of securing listings) are being unbelievably overlooked by most in our Industry and, I should say, for those reading this chapter, even if ten thousand Realtors® read this book, a million of your competitors will not; giving you an enormous opportunity.

As a result of my community-based differentiation, especially since I was provided the exclusive opportunity for my towns from TownAdvisor, I am securing listings at a level I could never have imagined.

(To see Julie Vanderblue's Real Estate Town Docu-Mentary℠ go to: TownAdvisor.com/FairfieldCT)

Gee Dunsten:

I agree with Julie. Other than telling a prospective homeseller "that I do a better job at negotiating and staging" (and who doesn't say this), what better way to differentiate myself than to announce to homesellers, "When I market an individual home, I market the value of the town as well, through my town-specific website and town video... as not only does your home compete against other homes, but your town/city competes against other towns. Therefore we need to sell both... and only I do this. Let me show you or send you a link regarding how I sell the value of your town."

The Real Estate Town Docu-Mentary℠ I produced for Ocean City is the single, greatest differentiator I have enjoyed in my entire career... bar none.

(To see Gee Dunsten's Real Estate Town Docu-Mentary℠ go to: TownAdvisor.com/OceanCityMD)

Jack O'Connor:

I used to try to differentiate myself regarding how I am different. Now I differentiate myself by how I make the homesellers' town different than all other towns. It sounds simple but homesellers respond to this shift in a huge way.

I shouldn't even be sharing this... but I will. The difference between an agent trying to explain what makes "them different" versus what makes "the town different" is like someone trying to sell you a house while all the time talking about how they love the house they live in. There is a massive disconnect between what many in our industry focus on and what is important to consumers.

> When I market an individual home, I market the value of the town as well through my town specific website and town video... as not only does your home compete against other homes but your town/city competes against other towns. Therefore we need to sell both... and only I do this. Let me show you or send you a link regarding how I sell the value of your town.

Since I'm the only Realtor® in Castle Rock who can have a Real Estate Town Docu-Mentary℠ produced, I'm willing to share this link so you can imagine what it would be like for you if you could also exclusively present this remarkable service to your local homeowners.

(To see Jack O'Connor's Real Estate Town Docu-Mentary℠ go to: TownAdvisor.com/CastleRockCO)

Pam Charron:

Without question, as much as I love Sarasota, and as much as I want to more comprehensively market all of my Sarasota area properties, I must confess that a major motivation in my collaborating with TownAdvisor (after being granted the exclusive rights to Sarasota to produce the Real Estate Town Docu-Mentary℠), was to differentiate myself, so that more homeowners would want me to market their property... along with their city.

Let's face it, many homesellers think that almost any Real Estate Professional can list or market their home... and some even think they can do it themselves.

What they do not believe is that all Real Estate Professionals can also professionally market the town or city they live in... nor do they think that they can do this; nor do they want to put in the effort (to market the entire town or city). This is because they are trying to "sell something"... but we are "marketing people" which also includes the overall community. Therefore, this is the most compelling way to immediately, and I mean immediately, differentiate yourself to both get more listing appointments and secure more listings.

(To see Pam Charrons's Real Estate Town Docu-Mentary[SM] go to: TownAdvisor.com/SarasotaFL)

A. Dalton:

I remember when I was at Realtor.com, that the early adopters of the practice of enhancing listings and acquiring featured home-positioning on our site dramatically increased their incomes.

Do you see the same happening here?

You are among the pioneers of community marketing and others will follow.

J. Vanderblue:

No, not when it comes to "community video" and here are my reasons.

First, the decision to enhance listings was mostly a decision to spend a little more money and with very little to do beyond that. In terms of adopting a different mindset, it was as simple as "let me go from one photo to many" versus "the marketing of a home" now evolving to "the marketing of an entire town."

Properly producing a community video requires a far deeper commitment to the development of the product: collaborating on a theme, developing a town or city narrative, determining a video shooting strategy, determining a town prioritization strategy, and much more.

Many in our Industry are not that strategic when it comes to marketing. Others do not live in a world of continuous enthusiasm.

In order to produce a product that the entire town will rally behind requires a strategy, enthusiasm, and a type of person who gets very excited about selling something other than themselves.

G. Dunsten:

I agree with everything Julie just said. Many in our business were forced into enhancing their listings, either because homeowners asked for it or because they learned that their competitors were winning listings because they made this a differentiator.

172

It will be years before homeowners demand that their Realtor® also make a community video as part of their marketing plan for their home. Accordingly, all those who are reactive will wait years. The few who are proactive (by bringing to the attention of homesellers both during marketing presentations and, more importantly, during listing appointments as the number one method of securing listings) will be the ones who will be the early adopters... and reap all the rewards.

J. O'Connor:

I completely agree. We are not the most strategic of professions. If we were, then the following questions would be commonplace:

• If I were selling my home, would I be impressed if my Realtor® marketed my home and town with the same level of precision and care given to each property?
• If I explained to homeowners that this was part of my standard marketing program, would I get more listings?
• How can I get this accomplished as economically and effectively as possible?
• How can I let all local homeowners know I have done this for the community?

P. Charron:

I must confess, I don't mind in the least that ninety-nine percent of my competitors can not invite someone to go online and see the way in which they are selling the virtues of living in Sarasota... but now I can and do. And, if anyone in our Industry comes up with a more relevant message to share with town residents, please let me know.

I also think thousands of additional videos have been attempted, but the way they are done leaves many with no other choice but to not share them with the world... and unfortunately, they are not even funny enough to become hits on YouTube.

And, of course, community videos should not be funny, as they are paying tribute to where individuals and families call home.

A. Dalton:

Well, since our panel is titled "The Don'ts and Do's of Producing a Community Video," let's move onto the Don'ts.

J. Vanderblue:

DON'T be the actor/actress in the video, be a co-producer and co-director. I say this as a former model (many years ago) and one who performed in front of the camera.

DON'T pay more than $5,000 to $10,000 tops, for an entire town or city – which should include ground and aerial video, music, narration, script, development, press release, DVD or flash drive handouts, and marketing materials.
If your town is still available through TownAdvisor, grab it. You'll forever thank me. If your town isn't still available, find a way to get this done.

G. Dunsten:

DON'T include people's homes without permission.

Make sure you have a balance of video and captivating stills.

Certain scripts in certain places lend themselves better to movement, while others complement stationary photos. This is a real science.

J. O'Connor:

DON'T make the mistake of selecting someone to produce your video just because they can shoot video footage. Why do you think, when movie credits roll, the producer, director or writer's name comes before the camera man or woman's name? It's because this is not what they do.

DON'T have video shot and then write a script to coordinate with the visual. Just as with a movie, the script comes first.

DON'T look for a great writer. Instead seek someone with proven ability to not just write about a town, but to "sell the town." That's what town residents want and deserve.

> DON'T be the actor/actress in the video, be a co-producer and co-director. I say this as a former model (many years ago) and one who performed in front of the camera.

Most writers are not good salespeople and most good salespeople are not good writers; with TownAdvisor you get both... and exclusively.

P. Charron:

DON'T develop a script with your writer or co-writer based upon your interests alone. For example, someone who love sports but not the theater, might slant their town video too much towards athletics and recreation versus culture.

Make sure your producer researches the community interests of all demographics, in order to achieve proper proportionality.

A. Dalton:
How long a video do you recommend for the buyers and homesellers you seek to serve and impress?

J. Vanderblue:
Allan, your question drives the answer. I learned the hard way that you need to be clear as to "who your audience is."

Specifically, since I researched length of desired video online, and saw that videos should be around two minutes long when shown online to casual viewers, I made the mistake of thinking I could do a two to four minute video.

I tried and it didn't work. While it was short enough to sustain the interest of those who didn't live in the town (and who would never be interested in the town), it was not long enough to offer any remarkable substance to interested homesellers and prospective buyers. Therefore, my shorter (but high quality video) fell flat on its face... because it wasn't long enough.

I was confusing a one to three minute video of a "backyard cookout" on YouTube, and a four- to five-minute video "on homes" that I do, with what is required to capture the essence of a town or city.

Therefore, if you're not willing to commit to several minutes or more, trust me, don't waste your time or money. To prove my point, I invite you to Google "Fairfield Videos" and compare them to mine; Google: Fairfield Town Advisor.

I completely respect these efforts, because I made the same mistake at first myself, in thinking that something this brief would be better. But, I will let you decide for yourself. If you agree with me, contact TownAdvisor immediately and see if you can exclusively market your town(s).

G. Dunsten:
To Julie's point, if you're going to claim to homeowners that you are "the best at telling the town's story," then it cannot be done in the same amount of time as you would feature a home on video.

Mine is a little shorter than Julie's because Ocean City is not as nuanced as Julie's towns.

We have a tourist community, a smaller, full-time community, a bustling boardwalk with attractions, restaurants, and golf courses, but nowhere near the level of detail that needs to be revealed when a town like Fairfield competes against Westport, Greenwich, etc. My advice is that you can have several minutes or more in length offline. Check mine out. If you think it's long, that's because you don't live here or want to move here. You can break your video up online into several little one to two minute snippets for the casual, indifferent online visitor. They can click and view more or less, based upon their attention span.

Trust me though, not one person in any of my towns, including the Mayor and all the homeowners whose properties I have listed, has complained about the length. They love it and enjoy showing it their friends and acquaintances. We've all been sold on the idea that the optimum video length is about two minutes, when in effect, an interested party will actually watch for much longer. My advice to you? Do as I always do... listen to what homeowners say more than your competitors.

J. O'Connor:

I must admit, I too thought that if a video was more than two minutes long, no one would watch it. I have been deliriously, pleasantly surprised.

My first showing created an avalanche of interest, including a local merchants group that has my permission to include my town video in their marketing.

Now that I have produced my Castle Rock Real Estate Town Docu-Mentary℠ (Google: Castle Rock TownAdvisor), which is the single most effective marketing idea of my career, I realize that I couldn't even do a video on just one of our communities in less than two minutes... never mind my entire city.

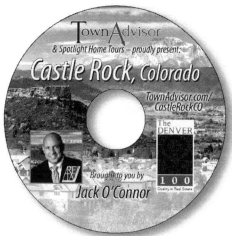

I now email and hand out DVDs (see picture) and flash drives at open houses, etc. and explain that I have done a several minute "mini-movie" on "Why Castle Rock is the best place to live in America." I am being swamped unlike anything else I have done in my entire career.

P. Charron:

Just as you would watch a ten minute video of your daughter's wedding, but not someone else's for that long, homeowners crave my Sarasota Real Estate Town Docu-Mentary℠. "Google it" and you will see why. (Google: Sarasota Town Advisor)

My video makes all my competitors appear indifferent or only able to market homes, not their communities, but homeowners realize that home value is tied to community perception.

Regarding length, one of my favorite T.V. shows is *Aerial America* on PBS. Each Video is approximately one hour per state. I would never have believed that the entire City of Sarasota could be captured (with what I call, "the town vitals") in approximately ten minutes of time. To provide so much detail, in such a short period of time, is truly a skill.

A. Dalton:

Well, the beauty of video is that the effectiveness surrounding it should, essentially, speak for itself... as we are able to view and hear it for ourselves.

That said, is there anything that any of you (as each of you has produced a highly successful community video) would like to share with our audience by way of summary?

J. Vanderblue:

I would like to make a couple additional points.

First, you need to work with your community video producer to develop a theme. For example, I know that, because Fairfield has two Universities, Allan, you decided the theme would be: "Fairfield: an Educated Choice." Homesellers have told me they love that because there are many towns closer to Manhattan and, therefore, Fairfield needs an overarching theme to cause buyers to travel further out to our town.

I know for Gee, Allan, you selected the theme "Is Ocean City a Town or City?" That entire video was about how it is the best of both worlds.

And then, for Pam and her beloved Sarasota, you selected "Sarasota: Where the Best in City and Resort Living Magically Meet" and, for Jack and Castle Rock, the theme that you and your staff and production team executed, along with Jack's collaboration was: "While a Man's Home is his Castle... in Castle Rock, a Castle is Everyone's Home."

I share this insider perspective with my industry colleagues because, while recently attending a workshop on luxury Real Estate at the National Association of Realtors® convention in New Orleans, I heard someone say, "Be prepared to spend up to 25 thousand dollars to do a first class video... and it will be well worth your investment."

Well, even though at twenty-five thousand dollars (doing what I have done) would be a great investment, I had my towns produced (with world-class videos) at more than an eighty percent discount. Check out my towns and let me know what you think and feel free to share with anyone heading to Metro New York.

G. Dunsten:

Allan, I know we are at the end of our time, but one more quick point. Before Town-Advisor scripted the Real Estate Town Docu-Mentaries℠ they produced for us, we were each asked to list all of the positives about our town or city and, interestingly enough, to also include any commonly-referenced negatives, as well.

In this regard, I cannot impress enough, the importance of the scripts.

For example, check out any of TownAdvisor's videos (a.k.a. Town Docu-Mentaries℠) and turn down the sound. You'll discover beautiful visuals, but virtually no impact with homesellers and buyers. That's why "the Talkies" put the old movie studios out of business. It's all about capturing the town narrative and, only then, using town images for support. Most Realtors® make the mistake of focusing more on the visuals. Huge mistake.

The fact that our Industry's "DNA" is more photo-oriented than text-oriented, is reflected in our history of classified abbreviations, such as M.E.I.K. Real Estate Town Docu-Mentaries℠ are driven by the narratives, since people are quite capable of driving around the town and seeing the scenery for themselves.

What homeowners want is for "the essence" of the town and its many nuances to be effectively conveyed. When they see this has been achieved in the town narrative, it becomes nearly impossible for them to list with anyone else.

A. Dalton:

Let me say that I have never enjoyed anything in my entire career as much as I have enjoyed paying tribute to where individuals and families call home... and I love how it also benefits one Real Estate Professional in each town or multiple towns.

Thank you for your willingness to not only share your community videos but to offer some "Don'ts and Do's" in general... and a behind the scenes perspective for all those who want to do community videos on their own.

178

Dalton Take-away:

These four legendary Realtors®have all gravitated to the concept of producing "mini-movies" (Real Estate Town Docu-Mentaries℠) versus merely "shooting a community video," because they possess a deeper desire to unearth and reveal what is truly distinctive about their communities in a much more substantive way than their ordinary competitors. They are therefore commensurately rewarded by homeowners who actually feel that their town is "a part of them" that's now proudly on display.

Chapter 20

<u>Creating Community Websites</u>
an interview with Rich Deacon & Thomas Ryan Ward

by Allan Dalton

Rich Deacon
TownAdvisor Web Developer

Thomas Ryan Ward
TownAdvisor Design Consultant

As I prepare for my interview with Rich Deacon, a front and backend Web Developer of national note, and Thomas Ryan "the designer" Ward, an accomplished multi-industry web and print designer, I updated myself on the "at-the-moment tally" of developed websites worldwide: 1 Billion, 217 Million, 434 Thousand... and growing by the second. Therefore, the question must be asked, "Does the world really need another one from you? How about your communities? Better yet, does your community really need or want a customized website about their community?" The answers are, "No, No, and a resounding, Yes!"

The reason why the community wants a website about their community (ie. town, city or neighborhood) is just that, "It's Their Community!"

I learned, while CEO of Realtor.com for several years, that only 1% of the visitors to our site clicked on "Find a Realtor®" and (surprise, surprise) they were Realtors® themselves! People are only interested in things that pertain to them... which should come as no shock to anyone.

The question becomes, "How much are the towns, cities, and neighborhoods where residents live important to them; either in terms of home values or town pride?" The answer is incontrovertibly, "Immensely!" And, if anyone would like to commission a survey that reveals a contrary finding (that being, that homeowners are not concerned about their home values and that town pride doesn't exist) to my assertion, please be my guest... and I will publish a correction.

Let's now review how you can separate yourself from your competitors (who merely post community information on their own, personal sites) by being prominently positioned, exclusively on a TownAdvisor.com Community Site.

181

Allan Dalton:

In your view, how important are community sites?

Rich Deacon:

I too am a believer that all things should be "local, local, local." The entire Web works from the knowledge that people want to "drill down" to gather hyperlocal, nuanced, and specific content. Just as those who search the Web for properties want particulars about individual homes, the same is true for those interested in accessing community data. As of yet, community-relevant content (from a lifestyle perspective) is just beginning to be effectively aggregated... which is required to provide relevant local content.

Ryan Ward:

I agree, with one caveat. Not only are consumers interested in accessing community-relevant facts and figures – over time, they'll also seek content based on the experiential knowledge of people who not only "eat in restaurants" within town or "stay in hotels" in the community – but they'll also want to hear what life is like living there from those who know best... local residents.

A. Dalton:

Question, "How important are pictures on local community websites?"

R. Deacon:

Allan, although images on their own (without highly descriptive titles or well-chosen Alt Tags) offer no aid in both search and SEO-ranking calculations, photos are a critical component toward user "stickiness" and increasing their time on site (or Bounce Rate).

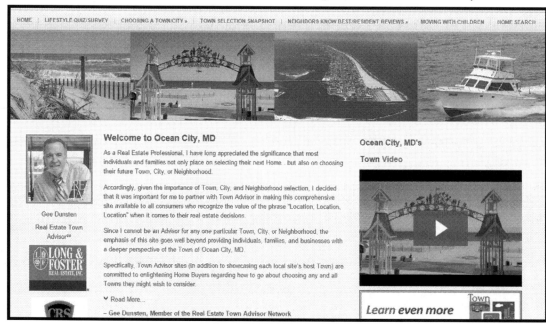

It's common web knowledge that articles or sites with photos average 94% more overall views. Look at Facebook, for example. Posts with images get over 35% more engagement than text posts alone. And, when it comes to eCommerce, over 60% of those seeking to a purchase a product say their decision is highly motivated by its image. Allan, unquestionably, people want to see pictures... and, when it comes to their community, this is no exception; I believe it is even more important!

A. Dalton:

In developing the TownAdvisor Community Sites, we emulated the Google Business Page photo carousel. Notice how Google places a photo slideshow above both search and organic results. Similarly, pictures at the top of Community Sites (whether a TownAdvisor created site or one our readers created on their own) are invaluable. Gentlemen, can either of you speak to the issue and importance of Consumer-Generated Content which Ryan referenced earlier?

T. R. Ward:

Allan, consumer-generated content represents the most trusted source for online advertising and all related advertising in general. Research conducted by Baynote and the National Association of Realtors® reveals that consumers are more likely to go to Yelp regarding their choice of restaurant instead of going to the restaurant's website itself. Similarly, people seeking to get travel or hotel information are more likely to go to TripAdvisor than a hotel's website. Consumers are convinced that the information they'll receive from their trusted peers online is far more relevant and unbiased than what they will receive from the hotels or restaurants themselves.

A. Dalton:

What did you do on TownAdvisor Local Community Marketing Sites, specifically, to accommodate the public's desire to comment (either in the form of Ratings, Reviews or Testimonials) and how do your Members deal with negative reviews?

T. R. Ward:

Both important questions, Allan. First of all, TownAdvisor sites offer a branded NeighborsKnowBest℠ TownTestimonials℠ component where visitors to our local sites can include text and photos (and soon video) about why they love their town. Our Members love it... but residents love it even more. Secondly, Allan, negative reviews on these local Community Sites are going to be few and far between.

The reason for this is that town residents are talking about the town they live in, rather than their stay at a hotel or dinner at a local restaurant. They don't "own" that local hotel or restaurant yet each resident understands that, by virtue of owning a home, they "own" part of the town. They are committed to sharing what is great about living there.

A. Dalton:

Thanks for that insight, Ryan. Rich, on the more technical end, how was the architecture for allowing for these Ratings and Reviews made available to both TownAdvisor Members and local residents across the country? Was this based on specifically-created coding?

R. Deacon:

Allan, the TownAdvisor websites, including their Neighbors Know Best℠ Town Testimonials℠ component, were built using standard CMS (or a Content Management System) which allows for the creation, editing, organization, and backend "upkeep" of that content in a central location. This is what many of your readers will understand as necessary in creating an online blog or news portal, etc. TownAdvisor sites also utilize custom coding and are built on highly scalable cloud-hosted LAMP stacks. Administration of CMS sites can be a challenge if the user interface is not user-friendly. By using a commonly known content management system like WordPress or Drupal, the learning curve can be significantly reduced. Using the WordPress CMS or Drupal also allows us to have a supported product with the upside of plugins and themes that have been tested and are industry-supported.

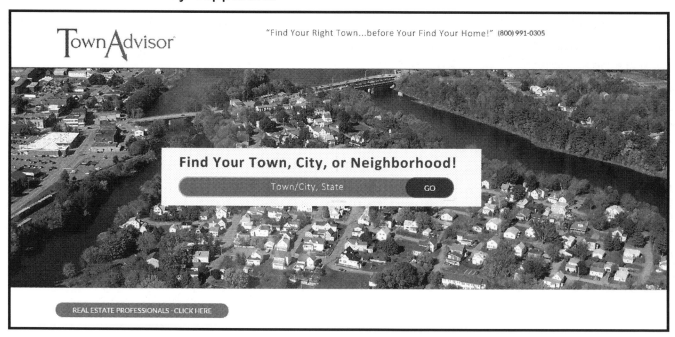

A. Dalton:

What's the difference between the TownAdvisor.com Town Portal and your Local Sites?

R. Deacon:

Allan, the TownAdvisor Town Portal is being built to allow consumers to connect to our network of Local Community Sites through a search portal. This portal will provide visitors with generic information about all towns, but the local sites will zero-in on detailed, community-based data, information, knowledge and wisdom.

A. Dalton:

There's a great fallacy that "if you build it, they will come." If that was the case, you wouldn't see sites like Angie's List and TripAdvisor advertising on television nearly every single night. How do your local members direct traffic to their local sites?

T. R. Ward:

Great question, Allan. It begins with our Members understanding that not only are the 30,000 residents in a particular town more valuable to their success than the 7 Billion that don't live in their town combined, it's infinitely easier and less expensive to reach, say, 4,000 local homeowners than elusive buyers coming in from all over the world. Our TownAdvisor sites and community videos (Real Estate Town Docu-Mentaries℠), through our local, branded Marketing System, are geared to securing one thing: Listings.

A. Dalton:

What do you say to a homeseller who asks, "Who's going to be seeing our town website and the local 'Documentary' you did for our town?"

T. R. Ward:

That's a simple one, Allan. The answer that can be provided by our Members is this: "Mr. and Mrs. Homeseller, every single buyer who comes to see your home through me (from open houses, advertising, my personal website, company website, co-broke, etc.) will all be introduced to both – as these are the only people we are looking to influence about the value of your overall lifestyle."

A. Dalton:

I love that honesty, Ryan, as it means that you are making a distinction between search engines (like Google, Bing, and Aol) and Real Estate Portals (like Realtor.com, Zillow and Trulia), and their role in bringing people to various towns – versus the role of the community website and video in strengthening the reason for someone not only to buy in that town... but that particular town and neighborhood.

T. R. Ward:

That's exactly right, Allan. To illustrate this point, I would like to offer our readers an analogy I have heard you utilize in the past, which I think is perfect. The way our Members view our sites is as follows:

Let's say a developer came into any of their towns and built a few hundred homes. That same developer then paid a local Realtor® to be responsible for the marketing of that development. Do you think that Realtor® would create a website and video of the development? Of course he/she would! Do you think the Realtor® would ask local residents for testimonials? Of course he/she would! Would the Realtor® do all this in-dependant of how much traffic that development website might receive from the web? Of course he/she would... and the Realtor® would be smart enough to realize that the reason he/she is doing all this is to further educate (at the end of the search path) those groups of buyers who are closest to moving to that community.

Our TownAdvisor Members appreciate that what they are now doing is marketing towns and cities through TownAdvisor websites and videos in the same way as marketing professionals market housing developments and communities for builders... yet in this case, they are doing so on a completely exclusive basis.

A. Dalton:

Ryan, that's exactly it. This is a great way for Members to prove to their community the following:

• That they're the most capable of capturing and telling the best story or narrative about their town, city, or neighborhood

• That their competitors appear to only know how to simply market homes... and not a town or city

• That their competitors are indifferent and, in an astonishing way, are suggesting that this is their way of saying, "I don't do windows!" But in this case, "I don't do towns!"

T. R. Ward:

Lastly, Allan, TownAdvisor (beyond our community-centric websites and Real Estate Town Docu-Mentaries℠) provides our Members with various tools to aid them in driving local residents to their exclusive town sites, including:

186

- What Do You Love about _(Town) Postcards (a call for TownTestimonials^{SM})
- Before Your Buy or Sell a Home_ watch the Real Estate Town Docu-Mentary^{SM} Postcard
- To Learn More about _(Town)_ Sign Riders (where applicable)
- ListingDiscs^{SM} (Real Estate Town Docu-Mentary^{SM} DVDs) or FlashDrives
- LinkCards^{SM} (Business Cards with Community Site links)
- Real Estate Town Meeting^{SM} Flyers and Brochures

The reaction we and our Members have enjoyed from these marketing products is overwhelmingly positive. Several are not listed here, as there are many more to come.

A. Dalton:

One last question. Many Realtors® want to know how IDX is being integrated into the TownAdvisor Local Community Website model. Can you both speak to that?

R. Deacon:

Allan, as you know, most Real Estate-related sites focus on listings and then agents offer some town or neighborhood information, thrown in merely as a secondary feature. The way for this first focus, listings, to be satisfied is through MLS/IDX-based systems to showcase listings. The MLS/IDX systems can be either custom solutions from feeds or third-party software or plugins that display the listings. The majority of these sites are cookie cutter with similar features and designs. Sites of this nature tend to have short session lengths and fickle customers, who use the sites purely as real estate search engines.

Our TownAdvisor sites include access to Realtors'® personal or company IDX feeds (via hyperlinks) but, as these are community-focused websites, they do not have an embedded IDX widget in the site itself.

T. R. Ward:

Yes, Allan, Rich is correct. The way that IDX access is offered in various locations (the top navigation bar, under the Realtor's® contact information, etc.) allows interested buyers a way to learn more about listings in the town but does not distract from the overall community celebration of the site. Additionally, Rich has added an attractive, pictorial Featured Homes slideshow at the bottom of each site which, similarly to the Google photo carousel-like town slideshow at the top, is complementary to the overall user experience and does not detract from the intended spirit of the sites.

Dalton's Take-away:

Once Real Estate Professionals accept the premise that all sites need to be promoted (in addition to ever-present SEO strategies), they arrive at this seminal question:

Will it be more relevant to local residents, when they are asked, "Why don't you come visit my website? I have information about all the towns in the area, including yours. Just go to Julie Vanderblue.com" or is it more effective to say, "You gotta visit the Community Website I had created that covers how great the town (either our town or your town) is to live in. Just Google: Town Advisor Fairfield CT."

I'm putting my money (as is Julie and others... even though Julie has a great personal site) behind promoting the community website, for this reason: It is better to promote a town site to the town (that exclusively features Julie but promotes the town) than a personal website that also features multiple towns. Personal websites are for all buyers. Town websites are for town homesellers and buyers who target that town.

Chapter 21

Ski Resort Properties
an interview with Steve Chin

by Gee Dunsten

Steve Chin:

Steve grew up in Sacramento, CA, graduated from Cal Poly-Pomona, and went on to work as a CPA for a top-ranked national Real Estate accounting firm, Kenneth Leventhal Company. In 1975, Steve and wife Val left L.A. for a short winter ski break that lasted 30 years in Park City, UT. Entering the world of Real Estate in 1980, Steve has found the business incredibly rewarding, and shares his vivacious dedication and passion with those he works with. Steve and his associates have successfully brought to market and represented over 20 developments within the area. They are highly respected among their peers, have a vast network of connections across the country, and are seasoned in all aspects of Real Estate.

Favorite Quote:

"Everyone has a right to how they feel, it's when you make judgment on those feelings that you create animosity." – Anonymous

Gee Dunsten:

Steve, when did you get into Real Estate?

Steve Chin:

It was in 1980. Prior to that time, I was a CPA for a number of years, working with a public accounting firm whose specialty was working with large Real Estate clients. One of my clients was Park City, so I made many visits to perform audits and do tax work during warm weather months. Although I was living in LA, I loved to ski, but couldn't go much because of tax season. After five years of failed attempts to get permission to visit our Park City client during the ski season, I finally decided to take the winter off and became a ski bum. To make ends meet I worked a variety of jobs from house cleaner to bellhop. At the end of that season in 1980, my wife and I decided to stay and we never went back to LA.

G. Dunsten:

How big was Park City then?

S. Chin:

Park City was a very small community with a number of established agents. That first year it cost me $13,000 to be in the business. In other words, I ended the year with $13K less than I started with.

190

G. Dunsten:

What triggered your path to success?

S. Chin:

I realized the importance of networking, as well as putting my accounting background to work. I started to provide assistance to anyone who was doing development and people who were looking at investing or trying to work out of an investment. I became more educated and began to offer myself as a resource for service clubs, small businesses, non-profit organizations, government bodies and committees, like planning and zoning. It's all about contacts and proving your value to everyone you meet in all aspects of your business.

G. Dunsten:

Steve, we've known each other for at least 20 years and you bring a lot to the table. What is your most important trait?

S. Chin:

Gee, it's empathy. Empathy is the most critical piece to establishing a long-term successful relationship. We must be able to understand where our clients are coming from, how they feel, and what is most important to them. It's a process of drilling down. What do they value most…

1. Money
2. Time
3. Green/Environment
4. Lifestyle
5. Ecology (Don't want a lot of noise or traffic)

Empathy can get you out of the Realtor® box where we're all painted with the same brush. Asking meaningful questions can be a game-changer in building relationships. For example, ask them what their favorite book is and why. I like to use analogies with my clients.

In the movie, Moneyball, Brad Pitt demonstrates the benefits of facts, numbers, and analytics. In our business, one of the first questions we need answered is where is our business coming from. What's our rate of return on the time and money we are spending?

G. Dunsten:

How about someone who is just starting out? What should they do to get a good start in a destination or resort community?

S. Chin:

Three things:

1. Become an assistant to someone who is successful. You'll get hands-on experience that's more valuable than something out of a book.
2. Learn everything about the cost and value of local Real Estate.
3. Know everything about your town or community.

G. Dunsten:

What are some of your most successful marketing activities that you would recommend?

S. Chin:

Create a *Red Book*. We developed and printed a book about anything and everything people might want to know about our community, from the history of the town to our personal recommendations about what to order at different restaurants, to where to find the best local craft stores. We had a great response to the book. In fact, they passed them out to visitors at the Chamber of Commerce.

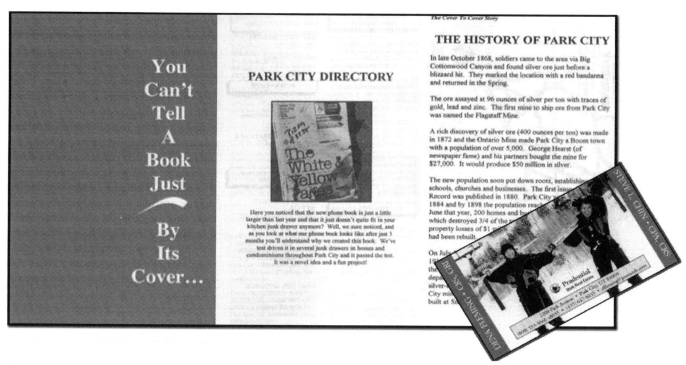

G. Dunsten:

How important is lifestyle to the sale?

S. Chin:

Gee, it's everything. 90% of the purchase is emotion. Park City started out as a ski area. We are now a huge year-round resort, so we sell all four seasons. In fact, we have different versions of our business card for different seasons. For example, a picture of our team getting on the ski lift or a picture of us putting on one of our picturesque golf courses during the summer.

G. Dunsten:
How do you get people together?

S. Chin:
Recently, we started doing a couple of out-of-town client parties targeted to some of our best customers, one in July and one during the winter. We send out announcements to save the date well in advance and then mail RSVP invitations six weeks before the party. So far, our attendance runs around 100 people (about 50%). It not only enhances our relationships, it peaks interest in what we're doing and generates referrals.

G. Dunsten:
Do you have any other tips or methods to grow your resort business?

S. Chin:
Allocate the time to network with local service providers in your community; people who are meeting visitors, seasonal owners, and newcomers throughout the year, such as:
1. Hotel employees (bellman, parking attendants, front desk personnel)
2. Restaurant wait staff
3. Favorite local shopkeepers
4. Taxi drivers
5. Airport pick-up drivers

For anyone in the service industry, a small, inexpensive thank you gift or extra good tip can go a long way and generates raving fans. One very cold winter, we passed out hand-warmers with our business card stuck in the glove to skiers. The key to top-of-the-mind awareness is keeping people engaged.

Don't overlook new construction. We've built a base of business by becoming an active, involved member of the local Homebuilders Association. I'd recommend going to their National Convention at least once every four years to keep up with the latest products and newest methods of construction. It gives us credibility with past, current, and future clients. We've also built a great reputation for getting other Realtor® members to cooperate and be excited and positive about selling our new home communities for our builders. We keep Realtor® members engaged in our prospective new community with a direct mail drip system throughout the different phases of construction. We send them little things in the mail like a washer without a nut to remind them that we are in our plumbing stage of construction. We might send a piece of wire with a note saying, *"Get a great charge and come by and see what we're doing!"* We might also send a carpet swatch during that phase of construction saying, *"We're getting laid next week!"*

Gee, the bottom line is you've got to be proactive in maintaining existing relationships and increasing visibility in your community. One of our key supports is Friends of Animals (FOA). The town hosts a pet parade in conjunction with Halloween and it's a great event, just perfect for kids, parents, families, and animals. The community aspect is FOA and Children (family and education component). I also believe that Rotary and Lion's Club are two of the best community organizations to be affiliated with.

G. Dunsten:
Steve, in closing, what is your favorite book and why?

S. Chin:
Four Agreements by Don Miguel Ruiz. The book talks about 4 key concepts to help us get through life. Two of my favorites are:
1. Don't make assumptions.
2. Don't take things personally.

The book shares how to work on these concepts and it's so well-presented and practical.

Dalton's Take-away:

Steve epitomizes the enviability and benefits of what occurs when one combines where one loves to live and what one loves to do, with their work in a way that the lines between work and play mesh.

While it may not be possible for all of us to "monetize ski-resort living" or "surfing in Hawaii," what we can do is this: look for all that we love in every town, neighborhood, city and region in which we work; from the diversity of its people, architecture, and (yes) even its changing weather. While some would say it is easier to have a high attitude in the high altitudes of the Rockies, the more positivity we bring to our career (wherever God has placed us) will benefit ourselves and all who are around us.

194

Chapter 22

The Role of Social Media
in Marketizing Communities
an interview with Michael Oppler

by Allan Dalton

Michael Oppler:

Michael is a Senior Vice President and Broker Associate at Prominent Properties Sotheby's International Realty, a luxury residential brokerage serving Northern and Central New Jersey. In addition to his role within the firm, he dedicates his time to the National Association of REAL-TORS® on the Strategic Thinking Advisory Committee, Chair of the Legislative Committee on the state level, and locally as a Board of Director. His interests also include advancing the goals of the REALTOR® Political Action Committee (RPAC) as an advocate for private property rights.

Favorite Quote(s):

"Sometimes when you innovate, you make mistakes. It is best to admit them quickly, and get on with improving your other innovations." – Steve Jobs

Allan Dalton:

Michael, when visualizing what our book, *Creating Real Estate Connections*, would speak to, I decided my greatest emphasis would be on hearing from people who, in addition to their so-called general practice, selected niche markets or segments from either their community or real estate community to specialize in.

While my greatest emphasis has been on local, offline community engagement, as the author of *Leveraging Your Links*, which was completely dedicated to online networking and social marketing, I also need to ensure that we do not overlook the greatest human-inspired juggernaut since the Gutenberg press.

Let me begin by asking you how you see the role of social media in terms of marketizing local communities?

Michael Oppler:

First of all, since your book is replete with mega producers from throughout the country who are generously sharing their best practices, I must say from the onset, that what I will be sharing will be largely influenced by my two professional associations.

First, I am Executive Vice President overseeing the departments of Career Development, Communications, and Marketing and Technology, of a twelve-office firm, serving the upscale marketplace of New Jersey, directly across from Manhattan.

Second, I have been selected to be the Vice Chair of the Strategic Thinking Advisory Committee for the National Association of Realtors®.

A. Dalton:
The other reason I wanted to include you in the book, Michael, is because I did not want to be accused of age discrimination. So, how old are you?

M. Oppler:
I am 28, which also explains my activism with the Young Professionals Network.

A. Dalton:
Let me start with what you can pass on to the industry from your extensive role as the eminent chairperson of the STAC, and specifically, as it relates to the future role and impact of ratings and reviews regarding local Realtors®.

M. Oppler:
It is not a question of IF ratings and reviews will become significantly more relevant in the selection process by consumers, but how soon and to what degree.

A. Dalton:
As I think you know, I was recently responsible for heading up a Yelp reviews response campaign for a major online company on a consulting basis and I must say, I am fearful that our industry, not always known for its communicative bedside manner, is not prepared to adroitly manage this ever-evolving phenomenon. What say you?

M. Oppler:
Allan, I completely agree, which is why the NAR® in its forward-thinking role, summoned a number of us to join in a task force designed to predict, plan, and prepare for our industry's inevitable need to properly respond, and also, to determine what proactive steps can be taken in the oncoming consumer tide of contents.

A. Dalton:
And what were the findings?

M. Oppler:
1. Industries and companies need to provide educational forums about how to plan and prepare to effectively manage ratings and reviews, especially those that are not kind-hearted.

2. Many companies need to reassess all of their communication as it relates to becoming more consumer centric.

3. Companies need to expand the duties of their PR, Communication/Social media

directors to serve in the capacity of instant online responders to both negative and positive reviews.

A. Dalton:

How do you believe that consumer ratings and reviews will differ between other industries and our own?

M. Oppler:

I think there will be one or two major differences that will drive future outcomes. First, according to consistent research, specifically the Harris Poll, real estate professionals are universally slammed. Therefore, a relentless barrage of disparaging posts will not be viewed as remarkable (or worthy of attention), but instead, will be viewed as predictable, and therefore, benign.

The second outcome will be that some industry professionals will make a science out of both influencing posts and leveraging positive ratings and reviews by sending links through prospecting, networking and client gatherings.

A. Dalton:

Let's move on from ratings and reviews to online marketing and your role as strategic advisor to arguably, the world's leader in online education, Grovo.

M. Oppler:

Allan, I'm glad you brought that up, because I do not see how any Realtor® can think that they can fully leverage the web without first enjoying a complete grasp of how it works.

In our haste as an industry to just post listings online and join social networks, many have not taken the time to develop a stronger sense of the underlying technology, architecture, functionality and purpose of various platforms, and Grovo is the easiest way for a Realtor® to immediately gain access to every aspect of the web, and especially Web 2.0, from LinkedIn to Facebook, Twitter, and Pinterest.

As it is, many of my colleagues around the country have been swept up in the migration to the web, but haven't as yet, created an integrated strategy to triage certain elements of the web based upon their current objectives.

For example, maximizing one's brand or visibility on the web should not take place without considerable research and forethought. We must remember that the web is not some huge farmers' market, flea market or convention exhibit hall where everyone has an equal opportunity to have their products seen.

A. Dalton:

So Michael, how does someone access Grovo and is it expensive?

M. Oppler:

Easy! Just go to Grovo.com and you'll see how remarkable the service is and the immense amount of value offered.

A. Dalton:

Would you also recommend Grovo to those looking for online review management?

M. Oppler:

Absolutely, and so much more.

A. Dalton:

What are the most common mistakes you see made by your company associates and colleagues as you travel across the country?

M. Oppler:

There are probably three.

1. Too many Realtors® conflate social media with social marketing and do not realize that in order to project value within your online community, your content must not only be real estate-relevant, but value- added. In other words, we must be adding value to people's lives, or to all consumers in general.

2. Another common mistake is the inappropriate use of certain platforms, such as social platforms, for business purposes. This is very seldom a successful strategy and in many cases actually repels your online audience. All you need to do is compare the number of likes generated by social content posted by real estate professionals (your Facebook friends) with those generated by business content posts.

3. Most Realtors® are satisfied with simply joining networks instead of attempting to lead or create their own online and offline network.

A. Dalton:

When a new professional joins your organization and asks how much of their business they should expect to receive from the online universe versus the local offline, how do you respond?

M. Oppler:

This is what I share with our new associates, many of whom have advanced degrees in law, accounting, and so on, so they seem to grasp the message quickly.

I tell them that there are two ways to generate business. One way is to try to buy it and the other way is to try to earn it. If they want to buy it, I put them in touch with Realtor.com, Zillow, Trulia, and other online lead- generation systems.

I also point out that the greatest way to do business in our industry is to first secure listings, because listings will generate buyers more than buyers will generate listings, and local listings that lead to open houses will generate more contact with local homeowners. Therefore, the bulk of their business should come from their commitment to earn it… through community networking, prospecting, and local event marketing and then in time, they'll develop much more business online from their offline success.

In fact, Allan, I tell them that you once told me that while you were CEO of Realtor.com, only 2% of consumers ever clicked on the "Find a Realtor®" feature and that the ones who did were all Realtors®. This reinforces the old cliche that listings are the name of the game, probably more so today than in any other time in history, because they overwhelmingly generate the best chance for consumers to contact you directly, instead of being intercepted by others who are paying for leads. Like in most fields, what is indicated is that all professionals should have a balanced overall strategy that includes working many sources, but zeroing in on specific specialty marketing, such as that which is described throughout this book, and then figure out if it's easier to reach this particular segment online or offline.

A. Dalton:

In general Michael, do you think it's easier to reach FSBO, Expireds, Seniors, and downsizers, offline or online? One would think it must be easier online, because every booth at a convention is about the web.

M. Oppler:

It's funny you say that. I think that is our industry's dirty little secret. Most of the top-producers in our industry are rainmakers in their offline community on the listing side of the business, but they are smart enough to take some of that money and invest it to increase their SEO and buy a greater presence online, specifically for buyers.

Dalton's's Take-away:

You can be more influential offline locally than you can be online globally.

Chapter 23

Creating Real Estate Connections and Referrals through Industry Associations
the Importance for CRS, WCR & CIPS
interviews with Anita Davis, Becky Boosma, and Robert Morris

by Gee Dunsten

Anita Davis:

A Baltimore native, Anita of Long and Foster Companies is a Director at her local board (GBBR), serves on local, state (MAR), & NAR® committees, (NAR® Federal Housing Policy Committee 2008-2009) & MAR Housing Affordability – keeping her up-to-date on the latest industry information. In 2013, Anita served as the National President for the Women's Council of REALTORS® (WCR).

Favorite Quote:

"Develop an attitude of gratitude, and give thanks for everything that happens to you, knowing that every step forward is a step toward achieving something bigger and better than your current situation." – Brian Tracy

Gee Dunsten:

When did you get into the real estate business, Anita?

Anita Davis:

I started in 1994. At that time I was a single mom looking for a career as an independent contractor so I could work my own hours and schedule. After exploring a variety of options, such as real estate, insurance, etc., I finally chose real estate, because selling a product that everyone wants and/or needs is not high pressure and I've always had a fascination with real estate. My career began with O'Connor, Piper & Flynn because they were a big company within the state of Maryland. The owners were all local and very hands-on in the way they ran the business and they also offered a mentor program for new agents. I was assigned to Judy Morris, who 12 years later, became my partner. After being in the business for one year working to develop my business, Judy came to me and said, "I need $85.00." (At that time she was the Maryland State Women's Council of Realtors'® President). Until then, she had never mentioned WCR. She said, "This is the organization you need to join. It's time to get involved and begin to give back to the industry that is giving back to you. Time to get to know the movers and shakers in our industry and that's through the Women's Council of Realtors®!" She put me on a small committee (holiday fundraiser for our Board) where she needed my help.

G. Dunsten:

How important is participation in some of NAR®'s councils or institutes?

A. Davis:

Everyone needs to get involved on a professional level. Involvement in anything that, by participation, brings some kind of benefit down the line helps us get to know people on a one-on-one basis, helps us build relationships that can help our transactions run more smoothly, and enables us to experience an exchange of values, which, in turn helps us grow and mature in our lives, communities, and businesses.

That February, I went to my first NAR® Mid-year Meetings in Hawaii with Judy. We roomed together which helped solidify our relationship and that was my first introduction to the Women's Council of Realtors® on a national level. What I learned and experienced was priceless and as a result, I have never missed a National meeting since.

G. Dunsten:
Why join the Women's Council of Realtors®, Anita?

A. Davis:
The Women's Council of Realtors® is about leadership. It's a wonderful format for any-one to use to build their leadership skills for involvement in their community, personal use, or in their business, as well as other careers. Our structured monthly meetings on a state or local level provide:
1. Professional education to help members increase their business
2. Networking opportunities to meet other professional agents
3. Relationship-building opportunities
4. A great opportunity to build and direct your leadership skills within the Chapter

G. Dunsten:
What can you tell us about what takes place on a national level?

A. Davis:
We are dedicated to supporting our local Chapters, because they provide the Council with a pipeline to what is happening on the grassroots level. Our focus is not to lose who they are, but to continue to gain greater recognition and credibility for women in real estate. We are committed to a 3-year strategic plan that is a living document. It continues to be reviewed twice a year on a national level and can be altered to meet a change in the industry and/or market. Also, our members report to staff with local and relevant information.

As a WCR past national president, I extended our commitment to…
1. Education – By providing more education and a higher quality experience for all different levels of member experience
2. Diversity – We need to fill or invite more diversity to the table. Everyone's point of view, regardless of background or gender is very important to our growth and continued success as an organization and as business people.

G. Dunsten:

Can men join your organization?

A. Davis:

Yes. If women only talk and listen to other women, they run the risk of missing out on a very important viewpoint. Just as men only listening to other men might end up with a more limited or narrow point of view. We have been reaching out toward more diversity for everyone's mutual benefit, so we welcome and need men's perspective at a table of women. Gee, our primary commitment is to advance women in our community. In fact, many of NAR®'s past, present, and future leaders were or will be women.

G. Dunsten:

Anita, what does the future look like for the Women's Council of Realtors® and NAR®?

A. Davis:

NAR® and WCR are making great strides within all of their societies and councils by developing great partnerships with each other. The bottom line is we all need to get involved! It helps develop our business skills, and networking can change our lives and careers. The key is to service our communities in the role of an advisor and resource.

Last spring, I was contacted by a friend who lives in Chicago who desperately needed to sell her condo that unfortunately, was still under water. She called me for advice on finding the right agent in Chicago for her situation. I selected a great agent and didn't ask for a referral fee, because the price was under $100K and I knew it was going to take a lot of work. After the property closed, the agent asked, "How can I repay you for giving me the referral?" and I replied, "The next time we're at NAR®, just buy me dinner and let's talk then about how we can do more referrals together.

G. Dunsten:

What are your closing thoughts, Anita?

A. Davis:

Our business shouldn't be about another paycheck. It should be about how well our client was served and about developing relationships that lead to other business. It's important to remind people that we are here for them in the role of an advisor or resource now and in the future. The transaction is about serving the client, not the immediate paycheck. It's not about getting paid today, it's about the rest of our lives.

Becky Boomsma:

Becky began her highly recognized Real Estate career as a top-producing Realtor® and speaker/presenter in 1998. Becky has served in industry leadership as Board Member and Past President of the New Jersey-Delaware State Chapter of CRS, a Board Member and Committee Chair of the New Jersey Association of Realtors®, and has served on several national real estate committees and on many within her local Board of Realtors®. She has been featured as a panel participant and presenter at many conferences and seminars, cited as a credible real estate resource and contributor for local and regional media television segments, a book, many news articles, and is with Prominent Properties Sotheby's International Realty.

Favorite Quote:

"Be the change you wish to see in the world." – Gandhi

Gee Dunsten:

Becky, how much of your business is derived from working with international clients?

Becky Boomsma:

International real estate business continues to grow. Currently, 45% of my clients are international clients.

G. Dunsten:

What attracts so many international buyers to your area?

B. Boomsma:

I think it's a number of things:
1. Proximity to New York City
2. Local colleges and universities
3. Location on the Atlantic Ocean

G. Dunsten:

What got you into serving this segment of the business?

B. Boomsma:

Gee, it's my interest and fascination with different cultures and my vast experience in traveling around the world."

G. Dunsten:

How have you become so successful?

B. Boomsma:

I've become a student of different cultures. It's important to learn about the different nuances, which will start at the first meeting with your client. The approach you take can build or destroy a relationship quickly.

1. How and when you'll communicate
2. Significance of family

For example, Hispanics are very family-oriented. It's their heart and their strength, so taking the time to get to know them and demonstrating a willingness to share backgrounds, can go a long way in developing trust.

Asians are more private. They don't show their emotions as much, however we must make the same commitment to get to know them and let them know something about us. Unless they have already had a lot of exposure to our American culture, we will have to be more patient and willing to spend more time in relationship-building.

In almost every situation, we must provide extra care, more time, more hand-holding, and more assurances. It's critical to understand that we really have to demonstrate our commitment to taking care of them and the real value we provide.

G. Dunsten:

What are some of the most important lessons you've learned?

B. Boomsma:

Our business shouldn't be about the paycheck. It should be about how well we serve our clients. It starts with investing the time to develop relationships. Strong relationships in the international world will lead to other business. The transaction is about serving the client, not the immediate paycheck. It's about the rest of our lives. If we don't tell people to use us as an advisor and remind them we're here for the future, also, they won't use us and/or refer their friends.

G. Dunsten:

Becky, what are some of the special services you provide?

B. Boomsma:

Great question. There are a number of challenges in working with international clients.
1. Differences in finances, based on their country
2. Differences in documentation, such as deeds
3. Potential for fraud when dealing with the disposition of property in different parts of the world

We must align ourselves with professionals, not only to reduce our liability, but to help our clients with issues like:
1. Getting their cash into the country
2. Dealing with immigration
3. Execution of documents
4. Streamlining the transaction

G. Dunsten:

What are some of the greatest opportunities available to capture international clients?

B. Boomsma:

You should be marketing to international consumers if you live:
1. In a resort
2. Near a university
3. Near a metropolitan area
4. In a comfortable environment, i.e., warm climate

G. Dunsten:

Becky, how can one get an effective start in the international real estate community?

B. Boomsma:

Go to NAR®'s library for information. Everyone should take the screening questionnaire for the Transnational Referral System, which can lead to admission to the International Referral Directory. Join CIPS (Certified International Property Specialist) and begin to take some of their classes. At the NAR® meetings, take the time to attend the CIPS and CRS international meetings. At the NAR® Convention, go to the Expo floor and visit the International section. All the different countries have a table with information and are assigned a specific time to man their table. Check the schedule to see when representatives from the countries you are most interested in will be available so you can talk with them. What a great opportunity to learn, network, and build relationships.

G. Dunsten:

What other strategies or suggestions do you have?

B. Boomsma:

You have to get out of your comfort zone. Think of it as an adventure. When you travel to another country, allocate enough time to stop in and visit other real estate professionals and companies. I always carry information about myself and my area/community in my suitcase to handout. Take the time to start building relationships on a personal level.

Participate in CIPS and/or the CRS international group. Everyone around the world looks at us, because they want to know how we run our business with such success.

There is a great future in working with international investors. Many are interested in multiple transactions or return to purchase another property.

Remember that they must love the community before they buy. It starts as a great place to visit and becomes a great place to live. Clients with cash want multiple family properties, as well as businesses. CIPS can be a great way to establish relationships and put yourself on a bigger stage.

On the next page: Robert Morris' interview

Robert Morris:

Robert is a keynote speaker, trainer and certified instructor. A broker with Bob Parks Realty, LLC, Robert entered the Real Estate business in 1985. Robert was honored with the Realtor®of the Year award at one of his local associations as well as Tennessee Realtor® Educator of the year. Robert is a Certified Instructor for CRS and CRB, a Course Facilitator for REBAC, and is also a PMN Course Facilitator/Instructor for WCR. He has conducted seminars, training workshops and leadership conferences for countless numbers of Realtors®, boards, conventions and associations throughout the continental US, Hawaii, Alaska, Canada, Puerto Rico, and the British West Indies. Co-Founder and President of Advanced Training & Seminars, Robert develops, writes and conducts numerous courses to meet the needs of Realtors® in the rapidly changing world of real estate.

<u>Favorite Quote:</u>

"We are exactly where we are supposed to be in our lives based on the decisions we have made or the lack there of." – Anonymous

---

Gee Dunsten:
Why did you get into the real estate business?

Robert Morris:
I was an only child. My mother was a school teacher, as well as, a real estate agent. After I finished school, she challenged me to take the test for my license. I did so and got my license in 1985.

G. Dunsten:
How did you find out about CRS?

R. Morris:
I found out about CRS while working with our local Association. Driven to succeed by continued challenges from my Mom, I took lots of classes on a local level, and while building relationships with some of the top local agents, I realized that most of them were CRSes.

G. Dunsten:
When did you get involved with CRS on a national level?

R. Morris:
In the early 90's, I became a GRI instructor. Pug Scoville, the Tennessee Association

of Realtor's® Head of Education at that time, and my wife, Kara, asked me why I wasn't involved with CRS. They said I had a lot to contribute and needed to get on a committee. While I was attending the NAR Convention in Hawaii, I met Nina Cottrell, the head of CRS at that time. She encouraged me to apply and audition for the faculty. I had the drive to be the very best and I discovered that CRS was an organization focused on attracting and making its members the very best group of residential agents in America.

G. Dunsten:
Robert, as a CRS leader and CRS instructor, what are some of the benefits of earning the CRS designation and joining the Council of Residential Specialists?

R. Morris:
Well first, Gee, CRS provides its members with immediate recognition as someone who is committed to excellence in residential real estate. CRS has created more awareness in the value of using a CRS in corporate America's HR Departments through the distribution of their Referral Directory. Second, CRS is all about providing leading-edge education for its members. The more knowledge, skills, and systems we develop, the greater our confidence and ability becomes, which makes it easier for our clients and customers to achieve their housing goals and objectives. Third, CRS represents the largest referral network in the industry, where CRS members are better able to match the needs of their clients with the very best-suited agent in the client's present or future community. Fourth, CRS continues to deliver updated, relevant information to its members on a weekly basis, both online and offline, in all aspects of our business. It's about what we need to know and do to deliver the very best service. Fifth, CRS members are more willing to share or give away their very best secrets to success, as well as, systems, tactics, and marketing materials. Sixth, the CRS structure of state and local chapters further enables greater opportunities to network and share ideas. It's an ideal way to create accountability partnerships.

G. Dunsten:
Robert, what is your secret to success?

R. Morris:
Get involved on all levels; nationally, regionally, and locally. Find an area that you're passionate about and jump in with both feet. You have to become more visible. To be more successful you have to participate. CRS helps its members stay more energized and excited about networking, so become more consumer-centric and stay involved.

Dalton's Take-away:

Anita, Becky and Robert all display the capacity to place ahead of their own self-interest, the greater good... a trait that automatically must impress their clients.

Chapter 24

Creating Corporate Relocation Connections through World-class Service
an interview with Pandra Richie
by Gee Dunsten

Pandra Richie:

Pandra is President of Corporate Real Estate Services for the Long & Foster Companies, the largest privately owned Real Estate company in the US. A twenty five year veteran of the relocation industry and with over thirty years of Real Estate experience, she holds both the Senior Certified Relocation Professional designation (SCRP) and Senior Global Mobility Specialist- Talent (SGMS-T) designations from Worldwide ERC, the global mobility organization.

Pandra has served on several national committees within the relocation industry and in the spring of 2010 she was inducted into Worldwide ERC's Hall of Leaders for her contributions to that organization. She served on Worldwide ERC's Board of Directors from 2009-2015 and in 2014 served as their Chairman of the Board.

Pandra has spoken at several national conferences, authored numerous articles on the relocation and Real Estate industry and has been honored as a lifetime member of Montclair's Who's Who in Real Estate.

Favorite Quote(s):

A community is like a ship; everyone ought to be prepared to take the helm.
  - Henrik Ibsen

Gee Dunsten:

When did you get into the Real Estate business, Pandra?

Pandra Richie:

It was after the birth of my first child in 1983. Before I got started, I went to my high school sweetheart, whose family owned an ERA franchise, to learn about the benefits of going into Real Estate. He told me in great detail all the negative things about the Real Estate business and why it was a bad choice. So, after careful consideration, I got my license in spite of him and for the first six months, I worked part-time.

G. Dunsten:

What brought you to the relocation side of our business?

P. Richie:

Gee, as a residential agent, I quickly discovered that I enjoyed being a cheerleader for my community. I've always been very comfortable driving clients around my town and selling the benefits of living in my community. Along the way, I was offered the chance to work primarily in relocation and before long another door opened, which enabled me to transition into the corporate side of relocation with a large company. From there, I continued to move up the corporate ladder with other companies, as well.

G. Dunsten:
When did you join Long and Foster?

P. Richie:
In 2007, I was excited to join Long and Foster. Currently, I am President of the Corporate Real Estate Services division of Long and Foster, the largest independent Real Estate company in the country.

G. Dunsten:
What are the benefits in working in that position, Pandra?

P. Richie:
There are a lot of personal rewards in getting people acclimated to their new community.

G. Dunsten:
What have you learned in working with relocation clients?

P. Richie:
First, there are a lot of costs, as well as time associated with relocation that people on the other side often don't appreciate. Our job is about providing a high level of service. People are coming into a new location with lots of unknowns and many misconceptions. They need lots of local assistance, like finding the right grocery store, pharmacy, pediatrician, school, etc.

G. Dunsten:
What does it to take to be able to effectively assist the relocation client?

P. Richie:
It takes lots of enthusiasm and energy, as well as wearing the hat of a Chamber of Commerce representative. You must have a massive amount of information about your area and the local business community and the ability to sell the community as a great place to live by educating them about the benefits of living there. It should be more about the benefits of living there and less about not selling the house. You must have a reservoir of allied resources you can call upon to help them move/relocate and make the transition easier for them. As a result, the family will open up the door to their world and be more comfortable sharing their frustrations, fears, concerns, and beliefs, which will enable you to better assist them in making choices and decisions. The end

result is that they will be so overwhelmed by all the things you are doing and providing for them that they will become raving fans in their new neighborhood, at their job, and at their Corporate Headquarters.

G. Dunsten:
What are some of the key things you should understand or recognize to effectively assist the relocation client?

P. Richie:
You must understand what they are going through. Often, it's not only a move, it's a job change. There are different types of moves:

1. Company-sponsored move to a new work environment

2. A new hire or new department move that involves a new location, new job, and new company or division (Talk about being taken out of one's comfort zone!)

3. Self-directed move

Most moves are not self-directed moves, so things happen quickly with little or no prior knowledge and/or expectation, which often creates denial, frustration, anger, and hostility within the family. The spouse loses his/her present home and friends. The children lose their elementary school and/or the teenager, who is currently a member of a sports team or a class leader, doesn't want to move. Not to mention the challenges of moving a parent or the trauma of having to leave someone behind.

Empathy, patience, and a willingness to commit to dealing with different degrees of adversity are critical in working with corporate relocation clients, as well as the military. The hours are long, the compensation per hour can be low, and selling or finding the right home for your client is only part of the puzzle.

Most relocation families go on the web to do their research. The Realtor®'s job is to help them interpret the information and provide more relevant, hyper-local content. We need to be their eyes and ears and become their local trusted advisor on housing, local community alternatives, and the Real Estate market.

G. Dunsten:
How important is local knowledge?

P. Richie:

It's very important to possess a great deal of knowledge about your area and community, and it's especially important to stay current on everything that is happening, as well as, when, where, why, and how it's happening. Your wisdom will be much appreciated by your relocation client and their employer.

G. Dunsten:

Pandra, how has the relocation industry changed over the last two decades?

P. Richie:

First Gee, the relocation industry is a lot more sophisticated. There are a lot more tax ramifications with regard to fees, as well as benefit packages/moving expenses for their employees. Relocation now falls under the Procurement Department instead of the HR Department in most major companies. They're looking more at the costs of the move and less about the warm, fuzzy issues of the family. Today, you need to provide a wide range of additional services through trusted allied resources and our partners, such as:

1. Moving companies

2. Appraisers

3. Household goods storage

4. Temporary housing

5. Spouse and/or family counseling

6. Property management services

7. Immigration service

8. Tax consultants

9. Disposal of their old home

G. Dunsten:

How important is it to belong to a referral network?

P. Richie:

The relocation industry is unique. It's such a relationship industry. It's everything. It's where referrals are formed. Our long-term success is based on the formation of personal relationships. The relocation business is big and it is also small. Whether you're with a major brand or an independent broker, becoming part of an affiliation of like-minded companies who can handle servicing the relocation client on the other end with trust and confidence, is huge. We've been a member of Leading Real Estate Companies of the World since its creation. In fact, Wes Foster, Long and Foster's founder and Chairman of the Board, was one of the original founders of Leading RE. It was created for independent brokers, which opens doors to great education and training, as well as networking at industry events regardless of the size, for all members.

G. Dunsten:
Pandra, what would you like to say in closing?

P. Richie:
Like in any other segment of our business, relocation is about trust, building bridges, developing relationships, and providing great service. You can't make a sale without being face-to-face and belly-to-belly. Also, we all have a responsibility to give back to our industry, so take the time to volunteer wherever you can and don't be afraid to provide leadership where appropriate. It comes back tenfold.

Dalton's Take-away:

Pandra, time and time again displays a propensity for praising all but herself: her communities, where she describes herself as a cheerleader, her company, the Industry-iconic Long and Foster, and the illustrious, Leading Real Estate Companies of the World. These are the qualities that lead corporations to look for Relocation Divisions where they can be guaranteed that the needs of their precious employees will be placed above all personal interest. These qualities are exemplified by Pandra, and of course, her organization.

Chapter 25

Marketizing Your Community:
Creating Clients for Life

by Allan Dalton
Co-founder, TownAdvisor.com & Former CEO of Realtor.com

I was (at the time) a sixteen-year-old, pimply-faced political advocate standing in front of Brighton High School in Boston on a cold and rainy November night. It was election night and I was proudly holding a sign reading: "Vote for Joe Timilty, City Council."

Normally, when one "works the polls" personal safety is not an issue. That night it was; at least for me.

A much older and considerably huskier worker in support of another candidate actually grabbed my sign in protest to my relentlessly imploring chants of "Vote for Joe Timilty" and threw the sign out onto the street, screaming, "You and Joe Timilty can go to _____ Hell!"

It wasn't that I worried personally about going to Hell, it was just that my entire time (during those months of campaigning) I was consumed with the idea of Joe Timilty going to City Hall – not "Hades." Thus, a bloody battle ensued, with him getting the better of it and with me being attended to at nearby St. Elizabeth's Hospital for a dislocated right shoulder... an injury caused by me using a rotator cuff for throwing punches instead of shooting baskets. This was the first time I can re-call (at least vividly) fighting for what I believed to be in the best interest of the community.

This long-remembered, traumatic night forever informs me of one thing: Since I was in-volved in this campaign one hundred percent without any consideration of personal gain, it suggested to me that I was willing to fight for the interests of others rather than myself. In this case, I was fighting for the candidate whom I thought would best help not only my five siblings, but also our entire community.

I begin this chapter (of a book replete with professional, practical, and present-day com-munity-based perspectives from a diverse range of highly successful Real Estate prac-titioners), with this personal reflection as a way to directly confront you with this seminal question:

• How willing (not physically but emotionally and professionally) are you to put the Real Estate interests of all local homeowners and the community at large in front of your own by metaphorically fighting for their interests?

It is a question that perhaps requires rigorous introspection. After all, if you are a Realtor® then, in most cases, your fiduciary relationship is to either your buyer or seller client and not to the community at large.

To the contrary police officers, fire personnel, and local government officials do not have to wrestle with this question. For example, police officers are sworn to protect and serve the entire community, while Real Estate Professionals are only obligated to "protect" the interests of their clients. These ethical limitations, when extended to only buyers and sellers and not the community, (to some) are quite convenient... as direct clients are their only source of compensation.

Real Estate Professionals, of course, are interested in educating their own clients. The question is: "Are you also willing to educate all community residents regarding their Real Estate need for information and advice?"

I emphatically assert that, for future Realtors® especially, there will be a direct link between content-share and market-share.

A "community-based, content rich, career transformation" would signal a shift from the perception of one being "only a sales person standing at the ready when transactions are imminent by a small minority of residents and prospective residents" to now assuming the mantle of "one who should be engaged for any Real Estate-related need within the community... at any time."

> The question is: "Are you also willing to educate all community residents regarding their Real Estate need for information and advice?"

Client representation and community Real Estate advocacy can clearly co-exist.

Specifically, it is quite appropriate to illuminate all community homeowners as to what they might do to elevate home values, while at the same time (and in that same day) represent a buyer client; and aggressively help them buy a property that actually reduces average homes sales prices within the community.

That said, what do you think would happen to your career if every homeowner within your community believed (based upon your behavior) that you were willing to dedicate your entire career to increasing their lifestyle satisfaction and home values... even when not directly representing them?

How do you think your community(s) would respond to such a professional mindset? Let me solve this Real Estate riddle: They would be deeply appreciative!

Beyond that, what would you gain if all homeowners were convinced that you were "the incomparable champion" when it came to "telling their *town* story" as part of how you "supremely market their property" when they become clients?

219

Specifically, how would it impress homeowners (within the town(s), city(s), neighborhoods, and developments you work) when they ask you (during a listing/marketing presentation), "How are you different?" and you now, rather than falling into a trap where you actually see this as an opportunity for self-focus, say the following: "Folks, rather than focus on how I am different, I would rather focus on how we can make your lifestyle appear as being the most distinctive to prospective buyers... You see, I do not compete against other Real Estate Professionals as much as your home and town compete against other homes and towns. Therefore, the way that I am different is how I will establish how your overall lifestyle is different."

This, to them, would mean that you are fighting for "community home values."

And then what would also occur in your career if buyers (considering moving into the community) learned that you were essentially "that Real Estate community's Advisor?" What if the information, data, knowledge, and wisdom you possessed about the community was widely understood to be indispensable... and even second to none?

In other words, while data is readily available over the internet, your keen, knowledgeable insights need to become viewed within the community as a vital component of all community-based Real Estate decision making.

Are you a Real Estate Professional who is ready to move beyond personal promotion and into community promotion... or, better yet, integrate the two as in TownAdvisor.com?

• Are you ready to analyze your addressable markets?
• Convert your community into a personal Real Estate Social Network?
• Segment community-based Real Estate needs and interests?
• Commit to a strategic business plan and resoundingly communicate to all community homeowners that you are willing to, again, "fight for the community's Real Estate Interests?"

Then perhaps you can begin to enjoy the community following that local politicians enjoy.

That's right, while many vilify politicians in general, Congressional incumbents get re-elected over ninety-five percent of the time, a loyalty factor completely foreign to Real Estate professionals. The difference? They have mastered how to market for and manage community sentiment. They live in a world of community-relevance.

> Rather than focus on how I am different, I would rather focus on how we can make your lifestyle appear as being the most distinctive to prospective buyers... You see, I do not compete against other Real Estate Professionals as much as your home and town compete against other homes and towns. Therefore, the way that I am different is how I will establish how your overall lifestyle is different.

The Real Estate Industry, perhaps not so.

The Real Estate Industry essentially is an instant-gratification, transaction-to-transaction driven culture. We have not, as yet, displayed the same level of community-centric, strategic thinking that others who seek community support do – which is ironic, for Real Estate Professionals are arguably the most physically embedded people within the community!

To some community residents it might appear that Real Estate Professionals make their community presence known more in an attempt to secure business (in order to satisfy their own financial needs) more so than addressing the serious Real Estate needs and interests of local residents. Consequently, upon receiving the ubiquitous "Real Estate Calendar," its little wonder that the intent is viewed by consumers as more of a "prospecting ploy" rather than a helpful reminder of what day Thanksgiving falls on.

Impeding higher levels of local influence between Real Estate Professionals and local residents is a pronounced shortage of Real Estate-related scholarship being directed to consumer-centric Real Estate-related community engagement. One explanation for this void is the all-consuming attention being paid in support of the thinly layered relationships that characterize online communication. Unquestionably community-based, meaningful, and sustainable contact cannot be satisfied through Facebook, Twitter, and other social networking platforms alone.

There exists an enormous opportunity (if one can resist being a pawn in the monetization schemes of online portals that deliver leads or, in most cases, costly inquiries) to elevate oneself to being "King or Queen of the Offline Communities" where you live and work.

Sadly, many in our Industry conflate "overall community involvement" with "Real Estate-related community service."

Ask yourself this question: "Is my best and highest use to the community volunteering to help with the Fourth of July festivities (along with residents from a wide range of other professions) or, as the Real Estate Professional within the community, showing all homeowners how they can elevate their home values?"

> Upon receiving the ubiquitous "Real Estate Calendar," its little wonder that the intent is viewed by consumers as more of a prospecting ploy rather than a helpful reminder of what day Thanksgiving falls on.

While I think you can – and should – do both, your greater and unique value to your community(s) emanates from your Real Estate skills and community lifestyle related knowledge.

221

You deserve a strategy to "get the word out" (over and above the din of calendars, refrigerator magnets, pumpkins, and the ever-present notepads) and instead or additionally, establish yourself as representing higher Real Estate-related importance and relevance within your community(s).

Education and coaching, in a form that does not violate one's personal nature and sensibilities, are long overdue. Specifically, education that shows you how to move from the widespread Industry refrain that you should attempt to create "customers for life" and into the richer relationship field that is dedicated to creating "clients for life!"

Let's leave the customers to the department stores and let us be the first wave of Real Estate professionals who imitate our other professional colleagues – doctors, lawyers, financial planners, etc. – who are able to attain, within their same community(s), "clients for life."

There exists an enormous opportunity (if one can resist being a pawn in the monetization schemes of online portals that deliver leads or, in most cases, costly inquiries) to elevate oneself to being "King or Queen of the Offline Communities" where you live and work.

Real Estate Professionals work too hard to suffer through the uncertainty of a life of searching or "paying for customers" who employ them to complete the last stages of a

Real Estate transaction versus enjoying a lifetime of professional security through the rewards that accrue by developing "clients for life" within the community.

Remember, attracting buyers (often times) is a "matter of paying." Attracting sellers is a "matter of earning;" but this level of earning requires learning. Beginning with learning how to *Create Real Estate Connections* by first conveying that you are willing to "fight" for the Real Estate interests of the entire community.

Chapter 26

Fighting for Your Communities:
Changing 'Ambush Alley' to 'Realtor® Respect'

by Allan Dalton
Co-founder, TownAdvisor.com & Former CEO of Realtor.com

Since this entire book reflects the real career experiences of each contributor versus abstract theory, I will again speak from my own real-world experience on the subject of *Creating Real Estate Connections*. Ironically, the first community I have selected to focus on is the one that you belong to the Realtor® Community. That's right. Specifically, how you need to be respected as a community and a "market" to those who serve you... along with what happens when you are not properly engaged. My hope is that perhaps by examining how you, as a Realtor®, seek to be respected and engaged, it might lead to a greater appreciation regarding how the community at large seeks to be treated as well.

My perspective is drawn from the several years I devoted to being the CEO of Realtor.com.

I was personally touched at this past year's National Association of Realtors® Convention when two high-ranking NAR® officials came up to me (on separate occasions) and each thanked me for my role in "turning around Realtor.com." But truth be told, and not surprisingly, the restoration, re-engineering, rebooting, repositioning (or call it what you will) of Realtor.com was due to the efforts of many.

Fortunately the illustrious Chairman of the Board, Joe Hanauer (the single most consistently positive force in the history of Move.com and Realtor.com), along with Dale Stinton, Bob Goldberg, and other National Association of Realtors® executives agreed that Mike Long (former CEO of WebMD.com) was the person to turn around Homestore... which he "miraculously did."

I am grateful that Mike Long showed faith in me as well to help reverse the fortune and destiny of Realtor.com. I find it most gratifying that my team and I were able to do so (along with executives from the National Association of Realtors® – again most notably – Dale Stinton and Bob Goldberg – as well as a number of brokers, consumers, and client-centric Realtors®).

For our part within the Realtor.com division of Move.com, what we (David Bay, Adam Leff, Marty Frame, Mona Beckam, etc.) did had everything to do with changing the Realtor.com culture regarding the community we served you... the Realtor® Community.

While Realtor.com currently shows immense respect for all Realtors® and broker owners that wasn't always the case. As I cite in my opening chapter, just as some Realtors® unintentionally offend consumers so too did we unintentionally offend many Realtors® in the early days of Realtor.com (but certainly do not do that now).

When I arrived Realtor.com's inside sales force (referred to before I got there as tele-marketers) were greeted with a series of overhanging "motivational" banners when they arrived at work each day that read:

"Ambush Alley."

Twelve years ago this suggested, but certainly not today, that "they" were not fighting for Realtors® but were in a battle fighting against them – and Realtor.com was losing the fight! Today the opposite is true, as Realtor.com and its executives all vehemently fight for Realtors® without question.

I thought back then that, "If NAR® leaders Dale Stinton and Bob Goldberg (or any broker or Realtor® in the country) walked into our building and saw these predatory banners what message would this send? More importantly, what message was this sending to our Realtor.com team, regarding whom they served?"

I immediately met with our entire sales force and, after forensically evaluating all past training (which included eliminating the video from David Mamet's *Glengarry Glen Ross* as the centerpiece of our hackneyed messaging where we celebrated concepts like: "Selling is a numbers game!" and "You have to take seven no's before you get a yes!"). I conceived of – and then led – a completely different approach to serving the Realtor® Community, beginning with the following changes:

1. Posting banners throughout the building that changed "Ambush Alley" to "Realtor® Respect" and "Realtors® are why you have your career!"

2. Standardized Realtor.com pricing and eliminated all "special deals," as I emphatically asserted that all Realtors® within that community should be treated equally.

3. Eliminated all automatic renewals, as I believed that the Realtor® Community should not involuntary renew, but instead renew due to individual and contemplative decision making.

4. Established the possibility for brokers to enhance listings by creating "Company Showcase," thus putting an end to separating Realtors® from their companies in the use of the site.

Illustration: Ward / Dalton

226

5. Aggressively advanced the notion that Realtors® are not "numbers." Thus, this is not a "numbers game," but rather Realtors® are our clients; whether they pay money or not.

6. Changed the name "telemarketers" to "Account Executives," who helped each Realtor® manage their account with Realtor.com, an account that was triggered by their hard-earned listed/marketed property.

7. Instituted that each call must begin with this question: "Am I catching you at a bad time?" to display immediate respect for each Realtor®'s time.

8. Coached our Account Executives that one "no" was enough and how to present a logical benefit to Realtors® to essentially eliminate most or all "no's"... or respectfully move on.

9. Instituted educational seminars to help Realtors® while converting Realtor.com from a product into a service, a system, and a solution for both the needs of their clients and their careers.

Moreover, we spent hundreds of hours where I brought in successful Realtors® and broker owners (along with the owners of RIS Media – John Featherston and Darryl MacPherson) who have a 30 year track record of showing supreme respect to the Real Estate Community) to speak to our Account Executives. This was so we could create greater appreciation and deeper connections with Realtors® and brokers throughout the Realtor® Community. Our Account Executives were made more appreciative of how Realtors® work on straight commission, play an important role in our overall economy, and were deserving of help in learning more about the web. It was important to stress that Realtors® should never be privately mocked due to any reluctance on their part to do business with us... or for not embracing the latest technology.

Resultingly, one of my happier moments at Realtor.com was when legendary NAR® executive Bob Goldberg acknowledged to me personally the monumental reduction in the level of complaints registered by Realtors® at our NAR®-monitored Service Center... regarding how Realtors® were now being engaged by my servicing team.

While it was clear to me, that while we still hadn't arrived at the standards that Dale Stanton and Bob Goldberg had insisted upon, we had clearly been emancipated from the days of "Ambush Alley" and now lived in the world of "Realtor® Respect!"

That was then. Today, I am happy to say that Realtor.com deserves the highest praise for the completely respectful and integrity-laden manner in which they honor all Realtors® and brokers. I am so excited and completely confident that News Corp (which recently aquired Move.com) will now help take Realtor.com to the greatest heights ever for the consumer and Realtor® communities alike.

And speaking of NewsCorp, later in the book there is a chapter devoted to how New Jersey broker Larry Vecchio provided inspirational leadership throughout his sea-shore communities in the aftermath of superstorm Sandy and let it be noted that News Corp was among the few American corporations to donate 1 million dollars to Sandy relief efforts.

The reason I shared this personal background perspective is that when I decided to create a tee shirt for the convention in New Orleans (some eight years ago) which read on the back: "Realtor.com has your Back!" It was my way of saying: "We are fighting for you so that technology works *for*... and not *against* you!"

I also am willing to share this perspective regarding my Realtor.com tenure (which is one I have never publicly shared before until now) in order to emphatically make what I think is a most relevant point in terms of *Creating Real Estate Connections* within your communities: That being that I wish to address how you respond and react to any negative reaction (if any) you receive to your efforts to more robustly and resoundingly engage members of your communities.

By way of illustration let me say that while at Realtor.com I faced acute community resistance... even threats (when I raised prices)... but never once did it deter me from exploring all of the ways I could help Realtors® keep their value high and help how broker-ages could shift and save time and money by migrating their media spend from off to online and how our site could better serve the consumers and clients routinely served by Realtors®.

The same attitude of fighting for those I served was also evident when I was president and co-owner of my former thirty plus office Real Estate brokerage.

Therefore, as you evaluate the scores of community-centric ideas and programs presented by your Realtor® Community colleagues throughout this book, put to the side all concerns of rejection and self-concerns. Move beyond that... even when blood-ied... and remember, "It's windy at the top!"

Many Realtors®, for example, will knock on doors within their community for a charity, but not for a Real Estate matter of importance to the community. In one case they think they are giving... in the other, they think they are looking to extract something. But when you are fighting for community interests all prospecting, marketing, and networking become a matter of community respect... versus community ambush.

Thus, please don't ever view FSBOs, Expireds, homesellers, buyers, developers, local politicians, and businesses as anything but part of the overall community that you are fighting for and connecting with based upon your profound level of community-based Real Estate knowledge and considerable professional skills. Each and every Real Estate Professional would be well advised to do this each and every day. By doing so, your community will clearly recognize and appreciate your community-centric spirit of intent.

I have devoted these final chapters to matters concerning the "why" behind further community involvement. Indeed, we should all appreciate that, at times, community residents feel as though they are being ambushed by Real Estate sponsored and unabashed self-aggrandizement and irrelevant content to their self-interests. This entire book is devoted to creating greater respect and therefore, more Real Estate connections through greater relevance at the community level.

Chapter 27

<u>Creating Your Community Business Plan and Selecting the Right Coach</u>

by Allan Dalton

Co-founder, TownAdvisor.com & Former CEO of Realtor.com

As we head into the last chapter of *Creating Real Estate Connections* you might be thinking, "Wow, I have heard both why and how various iconic Real Estate professionals serve and monetize elements of their communities from luxury to seniors, military to distressed properties, to For Sale By Owners and Expireds, to building major regional brokerages, and to seasonal markets along with Creating Real Estate Connections with community organizations, local businesses, and through networks within the National Association of Realtors®... Now what?"

Well, now the stories within the book must completely shift to "your story" as you write the next chapter of your career.

In fact, if you do not create a customized community business plan as a result of carefully reviewing this book – or at the very least commit to significant change – then Gee Dunsten, myself, and all of our accomplished contributors will deem this book a failure. After all, *Creating Real Estate Connections* is not a book meant to entertain or satisfy the need for a temporary escape or distraction from the pressures of life. This book only warrants your respect if it helps you, your team, or your company provide greater value within your community(s) and therefore leads to higher compensation.

For this to occur it requires a commitment for many to become more strategic in their approach to business. A strategic orientation, however, is more the exception than the rule in our Industry... and for an explicable reason. Let me explain...

I once asked an audience of a thousand Realtors® to raise their hands if, when they were in high school or college, their strategy was to enter the Real Estate business. Three people raised their hands; two of whom were from long-standing family brokerages.

I then respectfully asked, "If a thousand doctors, lawyers, engineers, accountants, police officers, athletes, or entertainers were all asked that same question... how many more hands would have been elevated?"

The audience seemingly agreed that there would have be a considerable number of more individuals from these other professions who would have displayed a more strategic approach to their careers earlier on. Therefore, this might suggest that within our Industry's DNA there is not a resounding "strategic gene" evident. In fact (other than how the National Association of Realtors® is very strategic) were a consumer to ask most major Real Estate brokerages on the phone to be put through to their R&D Department (Research and Development), this request might generate silence or confusion. Consequently, I emphatically encourage you to use *Creating Real Estate Connections* as a catalyst for your strategic thinking, which will then lead to your strategic planning.

In my previous book, *Leveraging Your Links*, I quoted General Dwight D. Eisenhower, and shall do so again: "In preparing for battle I have always found that plans are useless, but planning is indispensable". The importance of this quote is that strategic thinking must lead to strategic planning if, for nothing else, to eliminate all the things that one should *not* be doing.

I also quoted the German philosopher Hegel. Hegel stated that all significant change addresses three segments when considered retrospectively:

• That the particular change was necessary
• That the change was beneficial
• That the change required a period of adjustment

Please understand this, in the context of *Creating Real Estate Connections*: First the Internet and then the World Wide Web (introduced approximately twenty years later) was a necessary change to bring information to the world more efficiently. In fact, the founders of Amazon.com stated that their mission was to eliminate illiteracy in the world. To most, the change that The Web created has been beneficial to the world. Yet, regarding an adjustment period, here is what the Real Estate Industry might want to correct:

• That while the Internet is considered the greatest development since the creation of the Gutenberg Printing Press of centuries past, it should not be viewed as the end-all regarding *Creating Real Estate Connections*. There still exists (perhaps more than ever) massive opportunities to marketize local communities through face-to-face and other community-based contact and engagement.
• That the Internet much more significantly deals with the securing of buying-side leads than generating listing-side referrals. Therefore, there needs to be a correction regarding how the Web represents its best and highest use.
• That an adjustment period is also required, so the Industry can evolve from Social Networking and Social Media to Social Marketing:

a) Social Networking and Social Media do not address marketplace needs. This is why so many struggle to monetize their Social Networking efforts in Real Estate. Social Networking represents a solution to a problem that never existed. Therefore, it violates the definition of marketing. Simply put, consumers never were at a loss in their need to locate Realtors®. Which again is why less than 2% of visitors to Realtor.com clicked on "Find a Realtor®" (Realtors® themselves).

b) Social Marketing is utilizing the Web in a way that helps or resolves unmet needs for consumers and markets via community websites and relevant, actionable content.

This is where the focus needs to be.

Perhaps Jim Weichert, a modern day Zeus-like Industry brokerage leader, said it best in his testimonial for my last book, *Leveraging Your Links*: "Success in Real Estate hasn't changed over the years. It's still about connecting with customers, but how and where that interaction takes place has. The ultimate goal is connecting with buyers and sellers, face-to-face. After all, technology is great but I have yet to see anyone shake hands with an e-mail, blog, or tweet." I also love the analogy that the Sun is a force of unique power, but its force can be blunted by shade or sunscreen, whereas a far less powerful laser can bore a hole directly through us. The Sun can be likened to the Web, and the Laser analogy speaks to how Realtors® – both off and online – must adjust as they properly harness the Web.

As you review this chapter please be thinking of creating your laser-like focus toward *Creating Real Estate Connections*. Let's get started...

Creating Your Community Business Plan

Here are my recommendations for your Community-based Strategic Planning.

1) Foremost, accept that a community-based business or marketing plan represents just one part of your overall business plan. Think of it this way: Just as a politician has to plan for many things, with one of them being strategic thinking leading to a political campaign (which does not also include all of their staffing, administrative, and governance needs), your community marketing plan is just one element of your career.

2) Identify your Addressable Markets:

Define Your Geographical Marketplace.
These are the following towns, neighborhoods, or communities
that I will target for engagement, for delivery of content, and securing listings:

_____

_____

_____

_____

Define Your Target Price Range.

My target price range where I will direct special emphasis is:

_____

_____

_____

_____

Determine the Number of Households
which You Want to Reach and Influence.

*The number of households I will target, both in individual towns
and in total, of my region are: _____.*

Determine How Frequently You will Make Contact.

*I will make contact _____ times a week, _____ times a month, _____ times a year with
all of these households.*

Determine what Means You will Take to Make Contact.

Direct Mail

E-mail

Social Media

Event Marketing

Referrals

Door-to-Door Canvassing

Other

Determine which Civic Organizations You will Belong to
and Develop a Plan for Inserting Influence.

I will join the following organizations...and by when?

_____

_____

_____

_____

I will influence members of each organization by doing:

_____

_____

_____

_____

Where applicable *(TownAdvisor members)*
Distribute Links to my TownAdvisor Website and
Real Estate Town Docu-Mentary℠ in the Following Ways:

Open Houses

Expired Listings

Pre-Listing Packet

Door-to-Door Flash Drive Delivery

E-mail Blasts

Other

Creating Real Estate Connections Through Your Sphere of Influence

Remember, everyone talks about Sphere of Influence as if it is a complete concept. It isn't. Many have large spheres without influencing them.

Developing a Sphere of Influence is a two-step process:

• First, how do you build your sphere?
• Second, how do you influence the people in it?

Direct Mail

Regarding Direct Mail, I recently had lunch with one of my former Associates and, when I asked how she did last year, she told me that she made $800,000. I asked her how. She said 97% was from her 16,000 postcards per month. She paid less than $100,000 per year (due to a special Post Office program) and grossed $800,000. She (according to my way of thinking) is in "the Direct Mail business – which seems to pay more than the "Real Estate Waiting for Business-business."

3) Select or Enhance your Contact Management System.

I used to oversee Top Producer, an amazing system when used properly, but which loses impact when not properly understood or is in the hands of a Realtor® who can not impress new contacts when meeting face-to-face.

4) Determine how many hours a day/week/month that you will prospect within your physical and online communities.

I will commit to prospecting so many days:

_____ *days a week*

_____ *days a month*

_____ *days a year.*

5) Determine how you can be distinctive in all niche markets that you make a part of your niche marketing campaigns.

I have selected and prioritized the following niche markets and
will create a customized marketing campaign for each by the date shown:

_____Date_____

_____Date_____

_____Date_____

_____Date_____

Two Seminal Career Questions

The Dean of the Harvard Business School suggests that you ask yourself these two questions:

• What do I do that my competitors do... that I do better?
• What do I do that my competitors also do not do?

You need to build all of your community marketing efforts in the knowledge that you have effectively answered these two strategic and far-reaching questions.

6) What Merchandising (product or service packaging) must I do to package my value proposition for each distinct market?

List Niche Market	How will you package your value?
_____	_____
_____	_____
_____	_____
_____	_____
_____	_____

7) Which ideas and practices from this book will I now include in my Community Marketing Campaigns? _____
Which authors will I reach out to?

Creating Community Business Partners and Sharing Success
Julie Vanderblue – julie@vanderblue.com

Becoming a Luxury Market Leader
Jack Cotton – jack@jackcotton.com

Distressed Properties
Brandon Brittingham – brandon.brittingham@longandfoster.com

Strategically Servicing Seniors
John Riggins – john@johnriggins.com

Serving the "Celebrity" Community
Valerie Fitzgerald – valerie@valeriefitzgerald.com

When the State is Your Community
Rei Mesa – ReiMesa@bhhsfloridarealty.com

Military Clients
Alexis Bolin – AlexisERA@aol.com

Embracing Diversity
Teresa Smith – Teresa.smith@bhhsgeorgia.com

Local Community Organizations
Leon Lopes – Leon@leonlopes.com

Leveraging Your Local Media
Russell Shaw – russell@nohasslelisting.com

Out-of-State Buyers and Sellers
Pam Charron – pam@sarasotaandbeyond.com

Seasonal Communities/Second Homes
Linda Rike – linda@lindarike.com

Helping Communities Storm Back
Larry Vecchio – larry@bhnj.com

Unlocking Gated and Golf Communities
Jack O'Connor – joconnor@den100.com

Creating Community Websites
Rich Deacon – rdeacon@rdeacon.com

Ski Resort Properties
Steve Chin – steve@deervalleyrealestate.com

Social Media in Marketizing Communities
Michael Oppler – michael.oppler@sothebysrealty.com

Real Estate Connections through Industry Associations
Anita Davis – anita.davis@lnf.com
Becky Boomsma – becky@beckyboomsma.com
Robert Morris – ATSeminarsLLC@gmail.com

Serving the Corporate Relocation Community
Pandra Richie – pandra.richie@longandfoster.com

Distinguishing Yourself within Your Community
Gee Dunsten – gee@gee-dunsten.com

Marketizing Your Community
Fighting for Your Communities
Fighting For (and not Against) For Sale By Owners and Expired Listing Homesellers
Creating Customized Community Videos
Creating a Community Business Plan and Selecting a Coach
Allan Dalton – allandaltonconsulting@gmail.com

• Will I try to see if I can shadow any of the authors? _____

• Which new NAR® designations will I pursue? _____

• Will I commit to becoming a Certified Community Marketing Specialist℠ through the online course *Becoming a Certified Community Marketing Specialist...* leading to an important designation) in order to put into action new and tested ideas and then leverage this new credential? _____

(To learn more and register for the next semester, go to CertifiedCommunityMarketingSpecialists.com)

8) Which scripts and training are required for each market segment?

9) How am I going to hold myself accountable? Who will help me add to my overall business plan (my intense, more community-centric, value-rich approach to my overall business plan)?

10) Selecting a Real Estate Business Coach.

AND THEN THERE WERE FOUR

Here are my recommendations:

To me, there are four giants in the field of Real Estate Industry Coaching. I very much believe that, for anyone completely serious about reaching their potential and significantly increasing their income, their path will be quicker and more sustainable if they are able to benefit from the coaching systems of any of the following four gentleman. And please know that, as a feminist, it pains me to have to list only men but there is no question in my mind that if there were a Mount Rushmore for Real Estate Coaches (none of whom are in need of my endorsement) it would consist of:

Mike Ferry:

I think Mike Ferry has helped more individuals make more money (outside of Real Estate brands and companies) than anyone or any company in Real Estate history. Mike essentially invented business planning and coaching for the Industry and is to prospecting what Bill Gates is to computers.

Mike dedicated his book *How To Make A Six Figure Income In Real Estate* (to me) so clearly, I am biased. But well beyond our personal relationship I cannot argue with his incomparable impact on the destiny of "Top Producers." It is clearly second to none. What most people do not know about Mike is that off-stage he is one of the kindest, most generous, and laid back gentleman one could ever meet. Another thing is that I do not know of any other business person who has studied more, researched more, and read more books on success than Mike... nor one who has honored, listened too, and featured more Realtors® than he.

And that's the irony. No one is more dogmatic than Mike, yet his dogma all comes from personal experience, top producer success, and the world's greatest minds (of which he is one). His disciplines are all monumentally researched and proven.

Illustration: Ward/Dalton

Mike Ferry – Craig Proctor – Tom Ferry – Brian Buffini

I strongly suggest you "carve out" one of these coaches and their systems to keep from ever going "bust!"

– Allan Dalton

Craig Proctor:

Craig is the single greatest all-time example of someone who has done it at the very highest level – and can also effectively teach others. For Craig to be either first, second, or third within the entire World of Remax (at a point in his career) and essentially do all of his marketing for Real Estate business in Canada without ever pointing out his sensational level of personal success is quite remarkable. His completely consumer-centric approach is consistent with his vast research that documents that "consumers don't care about the success of Real Estate Professionals... but rather their own," which also makes possible your greater success. Craig has made a science of consumer-relevant content and marketing and weaves these disciplines into his accountability systems and coaching. Craig has invited me to speak as the keynote speaker for many of his national conferences. It's the only time I ever get standing ovations because, as I end, he always stands behind me and waves his arms frantically imploring people to stand up. I'll take it!

Tom Ferry:

Tom is not only a breathtakingly charismatic and pulsating speaker, additionally Tom – in the family tradition – has spent years of study (along with a fortune in research) from psychology to prospecting methods, to accountability models, technology, coaching, and has also endeared himself to both Real Estate veterans (who know they need new methods) and a whole new breed of Realtors® who have become his exclusive followers. They love him because Tom truly loves them.

Tom is the sturdiest bridge in Real Estate for linking the proven methods of the past with the innovation brought forth from emerging technologies and behavioral sciences of the present and future.

Brian Buffini:

I have only met Brian a couple of times, but I have seen this mesmerizing stage speaker in action and, much more significantly, have literally had thousands of Realtors® tell me that Brian has not only changed their careers, but their lives as well. His emphasis on building success through personal referrals stands by itself in the annals of the Real Estate Industry. He is Ireland's gift to North America's Realtors®.

Brian provides the best integration of career coaching with life coaching, as each segment of life must be in harmony with one another within Real Estate careers.

Allan keynoting at annual Craig Proctor convention.

Beyond Coaching

If I thought I could coach like these four coaching legends, I would use my own book as a plug. Instead, of coaching (or attempting to coach) I consult. Meaning, I focus more on uncovering the individual needs and strengths of companies and individuals and then work with them on customized solutions versus being engaged with ongoing accountability.

The only coaching I have ever done was with my own daughters: Ginnie, Becky, and Laura. Let me share what I did with them because, if you can find a coach that is as obsessive about your success as I was with my kids you will be unstoppable.

When my oldest daughter Ginnie was a junior in high school, she came to me and said, "Dad, I want to get a job this summer at McDonald's."

Here is what I told her: "Ginnie, Mickey D's doesn't need you. Let me tell you the company that does need you – the Ginnie Dalton Future Corporation. I am the CEO of that company and I would like to hire you as its president. You will get paid one hundred dollars a week for the following: every day you will train for soccer for three hours, then study your Verbal SAT material for one hour and then your math for one hour. You will also train your incoming freshman sister, Becky, during your three hours of soccer."

We made up accountability forms that she submitted to me every Sunday night to receive her week's pay, which, to her credit, she faithfully executed.

Coaching Results

Ginnie made the high school All-American soccer team and went on to play at Princeton, where she graduated from. Ginnie is now a mother of three and is a board certified Ph.D. in clinical psychology with her own practice in Connecticut. Ginnie's younger sister Becky and she not only teamed up to win the New Jersey State Championship together, but Becky went on to become a two-time All-American as well and graduated from fellow Ivy League school U Penn where she played soccer. And Becky, interestingly enough (once her six children reach the proper age), will be launching a business devoted to helping children prepare for college life and beyond. Regarding Laura, a budding track star before injuring her leg, she won national writing awards, and was accepted to Sarah Lawrence due to her brilliant writing, but instead went to and graduated from Boston University (as did my wife and brother). Laura had a terrible accident in her senior year of college and became paralyzed from her chest down... but look out for Laura – as someday her writing is going to reveal that there is someone in my family who is actually qualified to write!

For some of you reading this book, if this example inspires you to do something similar with your children or grandchildren, then that alone will be reward enough for me to have written this book (along with my esteemed colleagues).

All of us deserve to have someone who mentors and coaches us. Although I'm not a coach, I revere them... and perhaps you should as well. I was blessed to have been drafted by the Boston Celtics *(Google: Allan Dalton Pick Up Basketball)* and this was only due to a series of coaches who each brought out the best of me.

I respectfully suggest you hire a coach (either Mike, Brian, Craig, or Tom), and if you already have one, discuss with your coach some of the ideas in this book; as they are here to help you in every way possible.

An Idea for Those Who Lead Real Estate Teams

Typically, teams have a team leader and then, associates or acolytes if you will. My advice: treat such team members as individual partners versus teammates, which you can do without changing any financial arrangements.

Consider law firms. Attorneys have partners and junior partners (who drop the junior when they need to spread their wings in front of prospects or clients).

By announcing that "someone is part of your team" it might be construed as "they are not even ready to perform a career fully on their own," especially one which most consumers do not think requires "group effort." After all, some consumers think they can do it by themselves.

How to Make this Team Transition

The team leader creates an individual brochure with select team members (where just the two of you are featured as partners): seven teammates, seven separate brochures. This empowers each "team member" and elevates them to "visible partner" status. This also makes it less likely that they will ever leave your team. Otherwise, their career may be doomed by constantly appearing as though their career has been confined to a protracted "training wheels period."

This positioning satisfies team members who yearn for higher status and possible emancipation from where they are viewed as apprentices. Their much appreciated new stature can also countervail the epidemic of teammate defections. All this costs is common sense. Marketing presentations now become: "My partner and I versus my Team Leader and I..." Hello!

Julie Vanderblue elevates her team members by positioning each one as exclusive TownAdvisor Members in the specialty towns she selects for them, but they appear with Julie at times as well.

Showing a group of people as "a team" makes the team leader look more like a pied piper, while showcasing individuals as "partners" elevates your compatriots. They are your contemporaries and not your subordinates.

Why not have it both ways?

Advice for Brokers

Great company-wide exercise: Explain that your company is always striving to be more community-centric and stress the importance of the relationship between marketing and community-centricness.

Ask your Associates at office meetings to define "marketing." You will hear: Branding. Promotion. Selling, etc. Point out that: marketing means – first – determining the unmet needs of the market and community and then creating goods and services to meet those needs.

After explaining this, ask company Associates to make a list of all of the Real Estate needs which exist within their markets. What will happen next will be that you will find that many of the needs listed will be the exact ones covered in the chapters of this book: Expireds, FSBOs, First Time Buyers, Military, Seniors, RELO, Diverse populations, Luxury, Downsizing, Merchants, etc.

Then, challenge yourself and your company by asking yourself this question: What is either your, or the company's, solution to each of these consumer needs?

This begins the process of creating consumer-relevance, and therefore, *Creating Real Estate Connections* within the community.

For example, if some consumers either want or need to move up, has your company developed a branded move up system? Or, is it enough to just keep telling everyone, "But we have the best brand" or "We sell the most homes," so therefore, we don't have to focus on that area. I believe that leaders generate consumer-based solutions and then educate the entire company on how these distinctive goods, services, and systems can be brought to the market.

And one last suggestion to all broker owners and managers: As simple as it might seem, I have found in my own personal brokerage (and in years of Industry-related consulting and speaking) an astonishing lack of preparation among company Associates to skillfully, resoundingly, and convincingly answer this most simple question, "Why should someone list/market their home with you... and your company?"

Interestingly, and ironically, I see office meetings where visiting home inspectors (for example) come in to dispense vital information, yet this most important subject of why someone should list their home with you (other than in basic training before any experiential knowledge kicks in) goes largely unfocused upon for years to come. After all, it is so basic. Yet it's as if the entire company has this most seminal task nailed! That's right, the most basic way for Realtor® Associates to make money is to best be able to answer this question (which is why we include this in our online certification course).

How many of your Associates are extremely confident based upon what they say, and what you get to hear them say, when they meet prospective homesellers? After all, 100% of their income is based upon how they communicate.

Ask your Associates at a company or office meeting this question: "How would your career change if you thought it was virtually impossible to lose a listing when in competition due to your supreme confidence (not cockiness)?"

Now realistically that doesn't mean that anyone is ever able to do that (check out Russell Shaw's honest percentages due to his sheer volume of appointments and his "No Hassle Listing" packet in Chapter 17). But the point is not that "one secures every listing" but instead that "one believes they absolutely will."

Instead, we have many in the Industry who exalt, "I get 90% of all listings from presentations!" Yes, they secure nine a year from ten appointments... friends, family, and neighbors. Why? Because they lack complete confidence in their presentations. This prevents them from waging an "all-out marketing, personal promotion, and prospecting campaign."

Therefore when I ask, "How would your career change if you believed it was nearly impossible for homesellers to say 'no' to you?" I generally hear the following answers:

• I would do more prospecting
• I would contact FSBOs and Expireds
• I would knock on doors
• I would invest into Direct Mail, etc.

Thus, this exercise (either as a one-on-one or in a group) to me is the single most important discovery that needs to happen at each brokerage in America.

What I have done over the years is ask everyone to fill out a 3 x 5 card with their answer (and not to sign their names). Then I collect all the cards, read the answers out loud, and ask everyone to comment... and sometimes rate their responses. This is a safe way to uncover this massive, massive, massive company and Industry-wide problem. And to hear the outright cackles caused by many of the responses secretly stated by those who stand in complete ignorance of how irrelevant what they say is and truly validates the need to preserve anonymity.

For this exercise to occur, however, the company needs to be prepared to offer company and individually-based marketing presentations that can be customized.

As broker owners you must ensure that your managers possess this skill-set and willingness to coach in this area. Otherwise, it causes your Associates to need to learn how to make "Listing Presentations" by paying outside mentors.   This is where your company's role in the marketing value proposition might go underserved. This also leads to the notion that "my future listing success has little to do with my company."

A Word About TownAdvisor^{SM}

TownAdvisor.com is precisely like it sounds, a new and developing portal dedicated to helping Real Estate consumers learn more about towns, cities, and neighborhoods when they are in the process of moving and in advance of them searching for the right home and place to reside in. TownAdvisor^{SM} creates community websites and Real Estate Town Docu-Mentaries^{SM} in partnership with only one individual, team, or company per town(s) and city.

We would love to discuss TownAdvisor^{SM} with you if this is something you would like to be a part of. To do so, contact us by visiting TownAdvisor.info.

Please also feel to contact me if there is ever anything I can do to reward you for honoring our book at AllanDaltonConsulting@gmail.com.

I would be remiss to end this book without reiterating and reinforcing the very first words that appear in this book. That would be, at the top of the front cover where Mike Long (the former CEO of WebMD) states that, "Realtors play an indispensable role in society yet need to do a better job of communicating their value." I think you will agree with me that every page of this book has been dedicated to helping you, regardless of your level of success and experience, to enhance both your real and perceived value within your local markets. I hope that this Spirt of Intent resoundingly came through throughout the entire book... if so, *Creating Real Estate Connections* is all that I hoped it would be.

– Allan Dalton

Don't Just Segment, "Desegment" Your Market

The reason why I want to end *Creating Real Estate Connections* by pointing to the TownAdvisor Community Marketing System is that I believe it must be said that for most Realtors®, and in most markets, significant success can not be found by merely focusing on one niche market alone. In many markets the addressable market for For Sale By Owners, Expired listing homeowners, Relo businesses, military personnel, luxury homes, seashore properties, gated communities, etc. are not usually adequate to generate substantial results by themselves.

The March 2015 copy of the *Harvard Business Review* speaks to this by, in essence, saying that businesses benefit enormously when – instead of trying to serve a niche market – they identify an unmet need within a larger market. The publication cites examples of how Apple and Amazon (through iPad and Kindle) successfully did this and also how Delta airlines, which sought to create an airline (Song) dedicated to serving upscale professional women, failed and went out of business in thirty-six months due to this segment or niche being too small.

Often times businesses, as well as Realtors®, can fail miserably if they "select a market that is too small to be sustainable." Instead, success comes through "successful market creating strategies that don't focus on finer segmentation but instead "desegmentation" – by identifying key commonalities across broad swaths of consumers."

This is precisely what we have done with TownAdvisor. Specifically, we have desegmented all homesellers – whether they are young, old, rich, or poor and regardless of their professional, political, or religious affiliation – and have identified key commonalities which aggregate all homeowners into one very large, and again, "desegmented market."

The key commonalities are:

• All homeowners are concerned about their home values.
• All homeowners either take pride in the town, city, or neighborhood in which they live... or want prospective buyers (see home values) to believe they would be proud to live there.

It is on these two commonalities where TownAdvisor's market creating strategies and niche marketing meet – over and above how buyers look to select their town or city before their home.

I began this book (in my foreword) by calling attention to how Real Estate Professionals can much more realistically create Real Estate connections – not through portals but through engaging consumers within the community. The communities are ready to be appropriately engaged... now you are too!

BONUS Chapter 28

Staying Safe... Professionally
by Allan Dalton

Co-founder, TownAdvisor.com & Former CEO of Realtor.com

Again, as North America's most prodigiously photoshopped and publicly exposed profession (one where Professionals routinely meet and greet strangers at Open Houses and vacant homes... at all hours of the day and during the evening), Realtor® vulnerability is real. Thus, our Industry needs to take heed of the statistics cited in the book, *The Sociopath Next Door*. Specifically "that 1 out of every 25 Americans is a sociopath."

Now, before you go and speculate that since you have 50 Associates in your office, "who might the two be?" let me lessen your anxiety by saying, that if you thoroughly researched the profile and definition of a sociopath you would learn that the sociopath profile is the opposite of almost all Real Estate Professionals. Therefore, it is the Real Estate Industry that needs to be aware of potential dangers in dealing with a very small percentage of consumers, rather than the need for consumers to be wary of Realtors®.

The reason why I decided to add this bonus chapter is that the premise behind *Creating Real Estate Connections* is: "By strategically and respectfully increasing your community-based range, reach, and influence you can expect to be rewarded through attaining significantly elevated income... by way of greater community exposure."

This means that you (as a result of enjoying exponentially greater exposure and local fanfare) must become not "increasingly alarmed" but rather "better prepared" for the statistical likelihood that you will encounter individuals dealing with antisocial problems.

A prime example of how increased exposure can elevate risk can be found in the entertainment industry. Given that Hollywood is the epicenter of celebrityhood, it is not surprising that the first state to enact anti-stalking legislation was California in 1990.

Unquestionably, the more you elevate your profile within the community the more that additional attention becomes an unavoidable by-product. For example if, after reading our chapters on creating community websites or town videos, you decide to exclusively host these programs for TownAdvisor (as just one example of elevating your Real Estate profile within your market), your visibility should soar. Moreover, sending postcards (which encourages residents to post positive comments on your site), appearing in more ads, or even deciding to "canvass" door-to-door all place you in the middle of the community spotlight. Additionally, now that you will have more listings, your personal website will enjoy greater exposure and visits as well. This elevated activity is exactly what you want and you should remain completely enthusiastic regarding how positive this will be in your life.

250

First of all, the chances of any problems regarding your personal safety resulting from this increased exposure is extremely remote. Nevertheless, it is a matter that none of us should ignore.

As I do throughout this book, I will speak from personal experience regarding the threat of one's personal safety while in the line of work. I recall a most stressful episode I encountered years ago, not concerning a consumer... but rather, a professional colleague.

I will always remember what I was told by a smiling, very calm, charismatic young man who was one of my sales associates: "Allan, because you caused me to lose the spring sales contest, I'll be bombing your home. Don't worry though, as I'm going to give your wife and kids plenty of notice because they didn't cause me to lose the sales contest. Instead you did by giving that lead to ___. Allan, I love you personally. In fact, do you want to go to the ball game with me tonight? I have tickets. It's just that professionally you've destroyed my career and you must pay!"

At that time I was not familiar with terms like "sociopath" or "psychopath," or references to a range of other mental disorders. Since that time my daughter (a clinical psychologist) has more fully educated me on both. Perhaps however, if I had given even a cursory glance at psychological descriptions regarding these mental and social disorders at that time, I could have been alerted... long before this traumatic episode ensued.

Ironically, perhaps this gentleman thought I was a psychopath or con-man myself (not saying that he was). After he was released from a 60 day lock down in a psychiatric ward he told me that he was moving out-of-state. I calmly looked him in the eyes with a feigned look of pain on my face and told him, "_____, you have no idea how much I am going to miss you."

That said, I do not intend to make light of those with any social disorder afflictions. My defense would be it's just that I was doing everything possible to keep him from bombing my home as he "got out of dodge."

Although the statistical likelihood of Realtors® experiencing violence is extremely remote, The National Association of Realtors® is relentlessly and resoundingly dedicated to the safety of all of its members. This is manifested in their ongoing effort to educate Realtors® on the importance of safety. I encourage all readers to visit: http://www.realtor.org/topics/realtor-safety/10-tips-for-holding-a-safe-open-house, as just one example of their vigilance.

However, for your convenience (and given the immense importance of this subject), I will list 10 ways to observe the importance of safety as provided by The National Association of Realtors®:

1. If possible, always try to have at least one other person working with you at the open house.

2. Check your cell phone's strength and signal prior to the open house. Have emergency numbers programmed on speed dial.

3. Upon entering a house for the first time, check all rooms and determine several "escape" routes. Make sure all deadbolt locks are unlocked to facilitate a faster escape.

4. Make sure that if you were to escape by the back door, you could escape from the backyard. Frequently, high fences surround yards that contain swimming pools or hot tubs.

5. Have all open house visitors sign in. Ask for full name, address, phone number and email.

6. When showing the house, always walk behind the prospect. Direct them; don't lead them. Say, for example, "The kitchen is on your left," and gesture for them to go ahead of you.

7. Avoid attics, basements, and getting trapped in small rooms.

8. Notify someone in your office, your answering service, a friend or a relative that you will be calling in every hour on the hour. And if you don't call, they are to call you.

9. Inform a neighbor that you will be showing the house and ask if he or she would keep an eye and ear open for anything out of the ordinary.

10. Don't assume that everyone has left the premises at the end of an open house. Check all of the rooms and the backyard prior to locking the doors. Be prepared to defend yourself, if necessary.

• Sources: Washington Real Estate Safety Council; City of Mesa, Arizona; Nevada County Board of REALTORS®; Georgia Real Estate Commission

Psychopaths are largely defined within medical journals as having the following traits: better educated, organized, charming, more manipulative than sociopaths (who are unfeeling and potentially violent). Psychopaths are largely defined as those showing a pervasive pattern of disregard for the rights and feelings of others. Psychopathic characteristics are often more genetically based, while sociopathic pathologies are more due to early life experiences. Although both psychopaths and sociopaths are lumped into one description given by the Diagnostic and Statistical Manual of Mental Disorders (DSM-5) under the classification of Antisocial Personality Disorder, many professionals point to distinctions. One illustration is that it is said that psychopaths (more than sociopaths) possess the requisites to be a "confidence man" or so-called "con-man".

I suggest you read Edward Smith's book *Confessions of a Confidence Man* if you ever have doubts about a particular Real Estate connection you have made. Reading the six steps that con-men follow in their process will help you better identify con-men.

I wish I had done so some 25 or so (pre-Google) years ago, when one of my top associates wasted weeks of her life working with a purported "member of Switzerland's royal family." This "gentleman" told her that he, "Needed to buy ten homes within two or three towns (all for one million dollars) and they must all close on the same day... for members of his royal family for when they visited New York!" Today I would have advised her differently than my just saying back then, "____, I have serious doubts."

Stalking...

I have heard scores of accounts of Realtors® being stalked. While our statistics are not quite at Austria's level (where 81% of those stalked are women and where 86% of all stalkers are men), I believe stalking is something that the Real Estate Industry needs to be constantly on guard against. Reports must be immediately filed, especially given the vast exposure of our Industry's female population.

Please remember that stalking need not be at the level portrayed by Robert De Niro in movies like *Taxi Driver, The Fan, and Cape Fear*, Kathy Bates in *Misery*, or by The Phantom in the classic example of *The Phantom of the Opera* to rise to the level of immediate, deep, and reportable concern.

While research reveals that most stalkers are former partners (personal and not professional), there are still far too many individuals that carry a mistaken belief that the other person loves them... and they become obsessive towards them.

Lambèr Royakkers, a noted Netherlands ethicist, writes that, "Stalking is a form of mental assault, in which the perpetrator repeatedly, unwantedly, and disruptively breaks into the life-world of the victim, with whom they have no relationship (or no longer have). Moreover, the separated acts that make up the intrusion cannot by themselves cause the mental abuse, but do taken together (cumulative effect)."

• Source: http://en.wikipedia.org/wiki/Cyberstalking

According to Dr. Michael Weiner, one of America's top forensic psychiatrists, when trying to distinguish between somebody who is merely annoying versus a legitimate stalker you need to ask yourself two basic questions:

• Do you feel you are being stalked?
• Do you feel you are in danger?

Dr. Weiner goes on to say that when you answer these questions in the affirmative, you need to convey to that person that you want all contact stopped and you should send this important message in writing. You should also include that if additional contact is made, the police will then be involved.

Given the disproportionate visual presence of the Real Estate Industry on the web, versus most professions, Realtors® should also be mindful that, according to Cindy Southworth, the Director of Technology for the National Network to End Domestic Violence, that 25% of stalking victims are due to cyber stalking. Ms. Southworth also offers this important advice: "If you think somebody knows too much about your activities, it is entirely possible and likely that the stalker is misusing technology tools to surveil and terrorize." As I conclude this chapter (one which candidly, I hesitated to write as I am not a medical, legal, or law enforcement professional), I encourage all readers to share this subject (perhaps even more than you presently do) with your colleagues.

If even one reader avoids a threat, reports a transgression, or takes strides to feel even safer in their professional and very public career, then my hesitation will give way to certainty that I made the right decision.

Remember, concerns of safety should never, in any way, slow down your strategic and most warranted community exposure. These concerns should simply co-exist with your exercising proper care... as in all matters of life.

As you exponentially increase your community visibility, if you encounter anyone who (in your gut) you feel gives you concerns, immediately disconnect... as these types of individuals may well require a category of professional care that is outside of your expertise. Plus, the more Real Estate connections you can create the easier it becomes to only focus on productive, professional relationships.

I've also asked some of my fellow book contributors to share their suggestions from their vast experience on how to best keep you and your Real Estate colleagues safe:

Gee Dunsten, my illustrious co-author, offers these tips:

1. Always be on guard when you are in the presence of strangers (stay alert and extremely cautious).

2. When showing property and/or holding an Open House, have a family member or office buddy call you every 30 or 60 minutes to check on you. If you don't answer, instruct them to call the police immediately.

3. Never meet a stranger at the property without a buddy riding with you.

4. Identify unknown Real Estate agents (it's easy for someone to print fake business cards). Call their office to check them out.

5. Arrive early (prior to meeting a client or Open House arrivals) at the property to:

• Introduce yourself to next door neighbors. Ask them to keep an eye out while you are holding the meeting/Open House
• Become familiar with the home's layout
• Unlock all doors
• Turn on all lights
• Identify escapes from different locations in the home
• Open all window shades and blinds, so others can see inside
• Observe and determine the best backyard exit strategy(s)
• Unlock windows in rooms that are a distance from the stairway or exit

6. Never lead your home tour. Always direct and gesture where your clients should go. Let them enter each room and always stay close to the doorway/threshold of each room.

7. Don't allow anyone in your blind spot.

8. Be prepared to defend yourself:

• Identify and/or locate items in each room as potential defensive weapons (small lamps, umbrella, kid's baseball bat or lacrosse stick, rolling pin, candlestick, paperweight, soda bottle, can of soup, letter opener, etc.)

- Bring pepper spray
- Stay a minimum distance of 6 feet from anyone
- Keep your hands free, with the exception of your cell phone or a heavy clipboard
- Stand sideways to reduce exposure
- Remember, the thumb is their weakest place, if grabbed
- Don't hesitate to grab a finger and bend backwards.

9. Don't assume that everyone has left the premises. Check all rooms and closets before you lock the doors to leave.

10. When possible, take photos of car tag numbers (for any suspicious people).

11. Notify the local police that you are holding an Open House and ask if they could have an officer drive-by while you are there.

Pam Charron of Sarasota, FL (Chapter 9) suggests:

1. Keep your cell phone in your hand at all times (this is also good if you ever inadvertently lock yourself out of a property). I also keep a spare $10.00 flip phone as a back-up with me at all times. The batteries on these last several days.

2. If unable to have two people at an Open House (and you feel you will lose sight of the front door), put a jingle bell on the handle so you can hear it at open and close.

3. There are many free safety apps for your phone and some Supra eKey pads have a less than obvious button which, when pressed, will call a person you pre-select. This is a great way to ensure that the "persona non grata" has no idea you are reaching out for an emergency contact.

4. Only carry your car key, lockbox, and phone. Put any handbag in the trunk, locked.

5. We all like to look successful, but leave home any glitzy or expensive jewelry which could be an attraction.

6. Do not allow your car to be blocked in a driveway. I typically park on the street.

7. Most of all, trust your gut. If something doesn't feel right, it probably isn't!

8. If I am showing property to someone I do not know, and particularly if I am not able to meet them at my office first, I will use the power of the internet and Google them to get a brief glimpse as to if they are "real." Realtors® are researched every day by prospects who are seeking to select who they want to work with. The reverse works well for us too.

<u>Julie Vanderblue of Fairfield, CT (Chapter 3) suggests:</u>

I have a tent card at all my Open Houses by the front door that states: "Disclaimer: Security cameras located throughout the home and property," and I conversationally add as I chat and welcome the attendees something like, "I'm not certain if the cameras or nanny-cams are currently activated, I just want you to know surveillance cameras might be present." We always advise our sellers to consider that option for their own security. I try to keep it light, but this keeps temptation LOW and also lets predators know that they may be filmed.

<u>Michael Oppler of Bergen County, NJ (Chapter 22) suggests:</u>

Although our phones and their myriad of powerful apps aid us in multiple ways, always be aware that many social media applications emit geolocation data. Make sure you check these apps' permissions and settings to increase your individual safety.

Given the enormity of online exposure that Realtors® are presently experiencing (which shows no sign of diminishing), I suggest every Realtor® check out:

FBI: http://www.fbi.gov/scams-safety/computer_protect

FCC: http://www.fcc.gov/guides/how-protect-yourself-online

Reader's Digest: http://www.rd.com/slideshows/10-ways-to-protect-yourself-online/

The Boston Globe: http://www.boston.com/ae/books/gallery/cyber_safety/

Thank you Gee, Pam, Julie, Michael, and of course The National Association of Realtors® for providing sound safety advice geared towards "Keeping Real Estate Safe."

In keeping with the importance of this subject I have created a website: www.KeepingRealEstateSafe.com for all those who would like to add additional tips.

While I have had some Industry colleagues suggest to me that a basic part of Industry training should now include Tae Kwon Do or visitations from former NAVY Seal instructors, which may not be realistic, it is realistic and quite necessary that each Real Estate Professional remain vigilant regarding not only their safety but the safety of their colleagues.

I hope this chapter is helpful.

Check out these Services

The following books, written by Industry Icons, can also help you increase your Real Estate Connections:

- NAR®'s Profile of Buyers' Home Feature Preferences
- NAR®'s Profile of Home Buyers and Sellers

- Barbara Corcoran
  Use What You've Got...
  and all her other books.

- Mike Ferry
  How to Develop a Six-Figure Income in Real Estate

- Craig Proctor
  No BS Direct Marketing

- Tom Ferry
  Creating Certainty and Success in Any Market; an Interview with Tom Ferry and Tony Robbins
  and all of his other books.

- Brian Buffini
  Work by Referral Live the Good Life

- Dave Liniger
  My Next Step: An Extraordinary Journey of Healing and Hope

- Alex Perriello
  Ten Traits for Top Performers

- Gary Keller
  The Millionaire Real Estate Agent

- Danielle Kennedy
  How to List & Sell Real Estate
  and all her other books.

- Darryl Davis
  How To Become a Power Agent in Real Estate...
  and all of his other books.
- Floyd Wickman
  Should I Quit Real Estate...

and all his other books.

- Michael J. Maher
  7L: The Seven Levels of Communication

- Tom Hopkins
  How to Master the Art of Selling
  and all his other books.

- Stefan Swanepoel
  Real Estate Confronts the Future
  and all his other books.

- Krisstina Wise
  Falling For Money

- Jack Cotton
  Selling Luxury Homes

- Valerie Fitzgerald
  Heart and Sold: How to Survive and Build a Recession-Proof Business

- David Knox
  Pricing Your Home to Sell DVD

- Spencer Rascoff, Stan Humphries
  Zillow Talk: The New Rules of Real Estate

The following Programs can help you create Real Estate connections.

Gee recommends the following Real Estate-related Services:

In my 30+ years of Creating Real Estate Connections with North American Realtors® (in all 50 States), I have been literally besieged with inquiries regarding "which systems, services and solutions" (in my opinion or for what I have heard) are the most effective and, even more importantly, reliable.

The following are my measured recommendations of companies and individuals whom I am confident and happy to recommend.

Coaches I recommend:

I agree with Allan's "Big Four": Mike Ferry, Craig Proctor, Tom Ferry, and Brian Buffini. I, however, would add two more to Allan's Mount Rushmore, Bob Corcoran and Amy Stoehr.

Lead Generation (buyer side leads):

Realtor.com

Zillow.com

Trulia.com

Homes.com

TigerLeads.com

HouseFax.com

Estately.com

BoomTownROI.com

LetItRain.com

AgentMachine.com

Lead Generation (listing side leads):

AnnounceMyMove.com

InTouch

HobbsHerder.com

tpmco.com (The Personal Marketing Company)

HouseFax.com

AgentMachine.com

TownAdvisor.com (recently launched and, exclusively, 1 Agent per Town)

Creating Real Estate Connections
through Important Professional Organizations and Networks:

CRS* – Certified Residential Specialist
GRI* – Graduate, REALTOR® Institute
CCIM* – Certified Commercial Investment Member
CRB* – Certified Real Estate Brokerage Manager
ABR* – Accredited Buyer's Representative
CIPS* – Certified International Property Specialist
SRES* – Seniors Real Estate Specialist
MRP* – Military Relocation Professional
e-PRO*
Green
CCMS^SM – Certified Community Marketing Specialist

Direct Mail Companies:

ExpressCopy.com
HobbsHerder.com
tpmco.com (The Personal Marketing Company)
QuantumDigital.com
VistaPrint.com
MerrillCorp.com
SharperAgent.com

Market Data:

RealDataStrategies.com
KeepingCurrentMatters.com
CityBlast.com

Real Estate Media Companies:

RIS Media
The Real Estate Book
Real Trends
Inman News
DupontRegistry.com

Luxury Home Magazines:

UniqueHomes.com
DupontRegistry.com
LuxuryHomeMagazine.com

Contact Management:

TopProducer.com
MarketLeader.com
RealProSystems.com
SharperAgent.com
SalesForce.com
RealtyCommander.com
ConstantContact.com

Social Media Consultation:

Grovo.com
MatthewFerrara.com
SocialMediaExaminer.com
Saul D. Klein

Video Production:

New.obeo.com
SpotlightHomeTours.com
TourFactory.com
Homevisit.com
ThatInterviewGuy.com

Community Video Production:

TownAdvisor.com
SpotlightHomeTours.com
New.obeo.com

Video Hosting:

Wistia.com
Vimeo.com
UStudio.com
SproutVideo.com

Website Design:

RealProSystems.com
LinkuRealty.com
Realestatewebmasters.com
Unionstreetmedia.com
Placester.com

Community Websites:

TownAdvisor.com

How to Become a
Certified Community Marketing Specialist^{SM}.

I am most pleased to announce this exciting new and most relevant Industry designation.

To earn a (CCMS^{SM}) designation requires completing our eight module and content-rich online course.

The course will prepare you to identify and then maximize niche community-based opportunities *within your local market.*

Additionally, upon completion of this efficient and convenient online and interactive course – taught by a remarkable and illustrious faculty of practitioners and educators – you will become the recipient and beneficiary of a highly pertinent community-centric credential (CCMS^{SM} designation). One that local homesellers, businesses and community organizations will immediately value.

We are pleased to provide this online certification course in a way that it is economical, while respecting the busy schedule of Real Estate Professionals.

– Gee Dunsten
    President, *Certified Community Marketing Specialist^{SM} Online Course*

264

TownAdvisor^{SM}

.com (B2C)
&
.info (B2B)

The Industry's ONLY *exclusive on and offline marketing system,*
Real Estate-related third-party 'community' websites and portal
conceived by Allan Dalton, *former CEO of Realtor.com*

• Become more Community-centric by proudly and properly promoting the town, towns, or city you serve.

• Offer town/city residents (homesellers and homebuyers) proprietary TownAdvisor content – aiding them toward making important Real Estate-related decisions:
Moving with Children, the Don'ts and Do's of Town Selection, Lifestyle Surveys & Quizzes, Town Selection Snapshot^{SM}, NeighborsKnowBest^{SM} & ChildrenKnowBest^{SM}, Real Estate Town Docu-Mentaries^{SM} and more...

LEARN MORE at
www. TownAdvisor.info

e-mail – info@TownAdvisor.com

call – (800) 991-0305

265

Made in the USA
Middletown, DE
10 October 2016